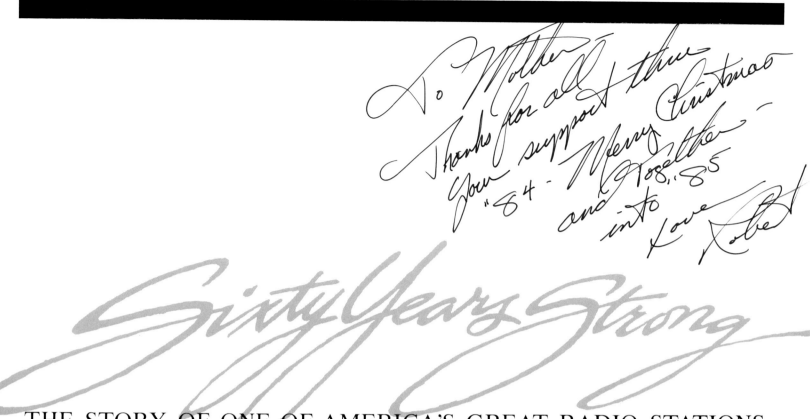

To Mother—
Thanks for all the
Your support thru
"84 — Merry Christmas
and Together—
into '85
Love Robert

Sixty Years Strong

THE STORY OF ONE OF AMERICA'S GREAT RADIO STATIONS
1924-1984

50,000 Watts Clear Channel · Minneapolis–St. Paul

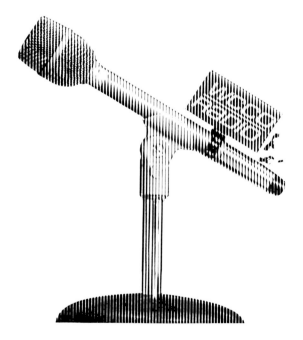

by Larry Haeg, Jr.

CONTENTS

The first-person accounts which preface each of WCCO Radio's seven decades in this book are fact mingled with fiction. Any similarity to real people, living or dead, is coincidental, although some situations are from real life. The 1950's story on the river resembles, in many ways, the girlhood of a good friend of mine named Mary.

Larry Haeg, Jr.

Library of Congress Card Catalog Number: 81-51631

This book is dedicated to the memory of the man who helped make WCCO Radio what it is today. After 60 years, still the Good Neighbor to the Northwest.
Larry Haeg, Sr.
1908-1982

WCCO

Radio and I have about the same date of birth. As a matter of fact, I am just a little older and have therefore known WCCO all of its life.

One of my earliest recollections is tuning the Atwater Kent radio that we had at home in New Richmond, Wisconsin to WCCO. The radio must have been one of the first because it had three tuning dials, each of which had to be tuned to the station before we could get the sound.

Since then I have regularly and religiously listened to WCCO for the news, information and entertainment that it has brought over the years and more recently, with pride that, as an officer of its parent company, I have had a very small connection with what has been a consistently great radio station.

People, not merely equipment, have made WCCO Radio what it is today. To them the parent corporation extends its thanks and congratulations on being *Sixty Years Strong.*

W.T. (Tom) Doar
Chairman of the Board
Midwest Communications, Inc.

W.T. Doar

Jim Rupp, President
Midwest Communications, Inc.

4

WE ARE OFTEN ASKED what makes WCCO Radio such a successful station— a true leader among the nearly 10,000 stations of the nation? Obviously, it is a combination of many elements. WCCO Radio boasts superb physical facilities with maximum power and coverage. Our full-service programming, based on a commitment to public service and community involvement, is the envy of the broadcasting industry. The same standards prevail throughout the other departments of the station.

To me, however, there is one ingredient that overrides them all. That is the *people* of WCCO Radio. Our staff. The on-air personalities and the technicians. The sales representatives and secretaries. Our news editors, promotion specialists, producers, receptionists, maintenance workers and the many others who team up to make WCCO Radio happen…24 hours a day, seven days a week.

I would like to use this occasion of our 60th anniversary to pay tribute to our entire staff—with special mention to those who have been with us for 25 years or more:

Irma Baldwin
Charlie Boone
V.A. (Buck) Buchanan
Dick Chapman
Roger Erickson
Bill Fuhrmann
Harlan Gabrielson
Sid Hartman
Art Johnson
Bob Johnson
Joyce Lamont
Al Loehlein
Gordon Mikkelson
Howard Viken

Two other people are uniquely deserving of our appreciation at this moment in the history of WCCO Radio. They are the two men who successively—and so successfully—served as general manager of the station for more than half of our past 60 years. They are the late Larry Haeg, Sr. who was our boss in the most beloved sense from 1952 until 1969 when he became president of our parent corporation, and Phil Lewis, who followed from 1969 until his retirement in 1983.

All of us at WCCO Radio look back on our history with pride… and, more importantly, look forward to the future with a sense of confidence and excitement. This feeling is strengthened and enhanced by the resources and support provided by our parent corporation, Midwest Communications, Inc., and its top executives—W.T. (Tom) Doar, chairman of the board, and Jim Rupp, president.

Thanks to the *people* of WCCO Radio, we are truly *Sixty Years Strong.*

Clayt Kaufman
General Manager

Clayt Kaufman

THE

20's

LITCHFIELD, MINNESOTA

We grew up on a farm near Litchfield in Central Minnesota in the 1920's, about the time radio invaded homes around the Midwest. Sinclair Lewis said it was "a good time, a good place, and a good preparation for life" and I'd have to agree.

Our house, as the saying went, was "six rooms and a path" (to the privy). The farm buildings were arranged like a small village protected by a battlement of grove and fruit trees and Norway pines. It was at once a fortress and a home, protecting and isolating us from the world. Then came radio.

In the mid-1920's, about the time we first heard WCCO Radio in the parlor, our house was still lit dimly at night with kerosene lamps. Rural electrification was 15 years away. Mercury vapor lamps hadn't arrived yet and at night the farmyards went dark. We had indoor plumbing in name only: a pump over the kitchen sink which drew soft water from the cistern, a stubborn contraption that gave water only for elbow grease. Just over the kitchen sink were dad's shaving mugs, razors and Bay Rum. We split wood and carried it into the kitchen to fuel the range where mom did everything from cooking sweet corn on humid summer afternoons to boiling water for butchering a hog. We had thick vegetable soup for lunch, roasts for dinner, home-made ost-kaka, head cheese and choke cherry jelly. She filled the kitchen with the aroma of fried ham and potatoes, green onions, beans, rice, and sauerkraut, pickles and salt pork from crocks in the cellar.

Our barnyard was a mosaic of sounds and smells, an animal kingdom, with giant draft horses under harness: muscular sorrels, roans and Belgians in their final, glorious era. Dad kept them til 1936. We had Duroc Jersey hogs, chickens, ducks, cats, assorted dogs of unknown parentage, and at least one mechanical beast, the black Model-T high enough to conquer muddy, rutted roads into downtown Litchfield.

I remember, as much as our first radio, the sour smell of silage, the leafy odor of packed alfalfa hay, the aroma of harness and pine tar, the sweet scent of warm milk in the cream separator. Over there, the back porch, where friends entered, a clutter of egg crates, carpet beaters, a wooden Maytag washer, winter coats and jackets, piles of wood and corn cobs for the stove. A child's life on the farm meant barrel-stave sleds, steel clamp-on skates, picking hazelnuts, home-made ice cream, quack grass and Canadian thistle in the fields, pig farrowing in the spring, never-ending chores and errands for which we gratefully received room and board.

Litchfield was a half hour's drive in the Model-T: a town of two-story brick houses, a general store, a frame hotel, a farm machinery dealer and the tallest point, a church spire. Dad and Mom were second generation Swedish immigrants, the first American farmers to turn from mere subsistence to dreams of prosperity. During the Twenties, Dad was one of the first in the Litchfield area to own a gasoline tractor, a milking machine, and an expensive radio. Like Henry Ford, he had a "puritan dread of anything involving debt." And that's probably what saved us. Land prices rose in speculation, so did farm

7

mortgage debt, so did the average size of family farms. More and more, farmers looked to the federal government for help. There were bumper crops but more bankrupt farmers. "The red lead paint peeled from the deserted barns," someone wrote years later, "sagging fences bore stark foreclosure signs, and the black Model-T's chugged off toward the city, overloaded with people and their poor possessions, like refugees in flight from the ravages of war."

We were lucky. Once in a while there was some money left over for luxuries. One day, much to our surprise, Mom said she had read about the new station in Minneapolis-Saint Paul, the "Gold Medal" station, WCCO, and how nice it would be in the evening to hear live music in the parlor. And wouldn't Dad need the latest market news? He sent to the Sterling Electric Company, Northwestern distributors for the Radio Corporation of America, for a free catalog. Several weeks later it arrived, for an extravagant $72.50, a new RCA Radiola RS with one stage audio frequency. Dad tuned it to WCCO, 500 watts, 417 meters, 740 kilocycles. He paid me the honor of being the first in the family to listen with the earphones. I will never forget the sounds I heard that night: a music recital sponsored by Purity Baking. Music had come to my ears 70 miles through the air, defying gravity. A black box had pulled sound down out of the winter sky. Our parlor had become a theater. Our world would never be the same. "Dad," I yelled, "Listen!"

The Foshay Tower, Minneapolis, 1929, the final stage of construction.

1924-1929

Sixty Years Strong

"We heard your station exceedingly clear and fine last night, set operating on one W.D. 11 tube. Signals and voice fine."

Mr. and Mrs. Lewis W. Fossieck
Saint Louis, Missouri

(listeners to WLAG, predecessor of WCCO Radio)

August 24, 1923

The Oak Grove Hotel overlooking Loring Park, Minneapolis, first home of WLAG, "The Call of The North." Below, WLAG Chief Engineer Ray Sweet. Right, in the beginning there was a dream, and the man who first uttered the magic call letters, WCCO, Dr. Paul Johnson.

WCCO

RADIO IN THE BEGINNING was essentially what it is now. A person. A microphone. An unseen audience. An invisible medium. Perhaps the most intimate, personal one ever devised by man. Radio is deceptively simple. There is less to it, yet more to it, than meets the ear.

During this one decade, stations like WCCO Radio helped create the first national advertising medium. They challenged, said someone, "the stability of the printing press itself." With radio, rural people became urban without leaving their homes, and vice versa. It was, said one radio executive, in 1922, "an unlimited theater, where rear seats are hundreds of miles from the stage and where the audience, all occupying private boxes, can come late or leave early...." It unleashed, to a great extent, the imagination of millions, who listened to music, drama and information, creating private images in the mind's eye. WCCO Radio was a part of this great national medium almost from the beginning.

It started not with a radio station but a company which made and sold crystal radio sets. Entrepreneurs Walter S. Harris and Mark Fraser, enchanted with this new medium, founded the Cutting and Washington Radio Corporation of Minneapolis in 1921, betting there was enough venture capital, as it's now called, among Twin Cities businesses to start a station and create a market for its sets. The gamble worked— for two painful years of nickel and dime skimping and primitive

Do-it-yourself radio: The crystal sets of the early 1920's— "A plaything for some, a consuming passion for others..."

11

The Wonderful World of "Willie-lag": studio, orchestra, and the stylish woman who ruled the station's early sound, Program Director Eleanor Poehler.

backed wicker chairs, overlooking Loring Park in Minneapolis. A temperamental but talented voice teacher and soprano from the MacPhail School of Music, Eleanor Poehler, became the managing director. Her fierce competitive instinct once drove her to try to prevent another station in town, WBAH (founded by the Dayton Company), from buying 250 watt transmitter tubes. She hired WLAG's first announcer, one of her best, young students, Paul Johnson.

It was, by 1984 standards, soporific broadcasting. WLAG claimed to have made Minneapolis "the radio center of North America...heard in every state in the Union, Canada, Alaska, Cuba, Mexico and on ships plying both oceans." In one 12-month period it received, it said, letters and telegrams from almost 43,000 listeners, from among other sites, Lake Champlin, Vermont to Butte County, California. What listeners actually *heard* on their crystal sets was quite another matter.

WLAG did not even own phonograph records. It had to borrow them from department stores which sponsored broadcasts. The records were broadcast by holding a carbon microphone in front of a Victrola. The music, at least at the beginning, under Mrs. Poehler's strict classical standards, was entirely of the potted palm, conservatory variety. The studios, if they were like others of its milieu, were probably like a "burlap-lined casket." For the first few years, at least, WLAG and its successor, WCCO, would not descend to popular music, jazz and what Mrs. Poehler called "the curse of the country fiddle." It was what William MacPhail

programming. Nine companies, including Northwestern National Bank and Donaldsons Department Store, helped pay the freight for the first year: operating costs of $35,000. Chief Engineer Ray Sweet flipped the switch and the rheostat that put WLAG, "The Call of the North," on the air with 500 watts at 9 a.m. Labor Day, September 4, 1922, from studios on the sixth floor of the brown brick Oak Grove Hotel, its ornate lobby with high, white ceiling, and sumptuous carpets and high-

would call "atrociously suggestive trash....jeopardizing the moral fibre of the American home." Mrs. Poehler even insisted on 15 seconds of silence to separate her lofty music from the vulgar spoken word. The delay came to be called "Willie-LAG."

Sports Broadcasting on WLAG was in its infancy too. Herb Paul reported University of Minnesota football games from old Northrop Field without the protection of a booth. He sat at a wooden table in the bleachers and stabbed a pocket knife through his hand-written rosters to keep them from blowing away.

The dream of WLAG blew away too, on July 31, 1924. It went off the air, practically bankrupt. Radio set dealers and distributors in the Northwest were back where they started two years earlier. Plenty of radio sets. Few radio stations in Minneapolis and Saint Paul to create a market.

In something akin to controlled panic, the dealers' association recruited bespectacled promoter Harry Wilbern. It was he who would hit the streets, knock on doors, and shake the business community until corporate support could be found to resurrect what remained of the noble WLAG.

This time, Wilbern had something going for him: timing. The United States, under the laconic Calvin Coolidge, had embarked on an unprecedented era of wild financial speculation, and a revolution in manners and morals. Radio was its darling. "Everything nailed down," said the Angel Gabriel in Marc Connelly's *The Green Pasture,*" is coming loose." Amidst ouija boards, cults,

bobbed hair, flappers, John Held cartoons, the dawn of the sexual revolution and the cosmetics industry, radio was the contemporary soundtrack. Yet it was also a comfortable companion, the "safe" amusement, for the far greater number of Americans who quietly raised families, built homes, paid bills, volunteered to make cities and towns better places to live. Spending on amusement and recreation in America in the 1920's would rise some 300 percent over the previous decade. In 1924 alone, the year WCCO Radio was born, Americans invested $358,000,000 in radio sets and parts, almost three times the previous year. Dozens of radio stations were being licensed each month, a communications revolution every bit as dramatic and far-reaching as the satellites, cables and VCR's of the 1970's and 1980's. Radio had universal appeal, for every social class, every geographic

"Directly ahead of us is a door leading into the concert room. Above the door a red light is burning and this is the signal that the transmitter is in operation. We cannot enter as any sound made will be broadcast by radio.

The light goes out and we enter the concert room. First of all it will be noticed that the voice has a very strange quality...the walls and ceiling have been treated so as to prevent any reflection of sound waves. Under the thick carpet are two layers of felt to insure that the concert room will be reverberation proof.

In the far corner on the pedestal is the very sensitive microphone which is designed to insure faithful reproduction of every graduation of tone of speech or music which is to be transmitted."

Ray Sweet
Chief Engineer, WLAG
in "Listenin' In"
the Official Radio News-Program of WLAG,
February 26, 1923

area, every race, every color, every creed. "No more," wrote one critic, "did the visible audience matter. Nothing mattered but that tiny black can......Present laughter now was nothing compared to absent laughter....it was the people you couldn't see—the ones you reached out there—who really counted. Reality now referred to something a step away from the original. Something you could neither see nor count nor thank..."

The Washburn Crosby Company of Minneapolis seized the moment and the medium. Its vice president, Donald D. Davis, perked up when he heard Wilbern's pitch. He convinced James Ford Bell, the company's engaging president, that radio could be a valuable marketing tool in Washburn Crosby's "flour war" with its major rival, Pillsbury. It must have seemed a hair-brained scheme to many conservative Washburn Crosby investors. Radio in 1924 did not make money. It consumed it as a fireplace does wood. Washburn Crosby, undaunted, bought the physical plant and assets of the former WLAG, kicked in another $50,000 a year for three years, then challenged businessmen in Minneapolis and Saint Paul to match it. Minneapolis gave $30,000, Saint Paul $20,000, and "The Gold Medal Station," using the old WLAG call letters, went on the air September 12, 1924, one of only 15 stations to broadcast General John J. Pershing's farewell address to the nation.

General Mills Vice President Donald D. Davis: "...we believed that anything so manifestly for the good of the public would somehow be good for us."

To reach a vast, unseen audience. Ground-breaking for the first WCCO Radio transmitter near Anoka, October, 1924. Left, Saint Paul Mayor Arthur E. Nelson holds the reins for Mrs. Sumner T. McKnight and Mrs. Edwin White and, below, swings the first pick into the soil of an old chicken farm. Right, Sewall D. Andrews, Minneapolis, WCCO's Henry Wilbern, and Foster Hannaford of Saint Paul, members of the board of control of "The Gold Medal Station" on that day of great promise in October, 1924.

Then, a day to remember, October 1, 1924. Clark Griffith's Washington Senators prepared to play John McGraw's New York Giants in the World Series. Sculptor Gutzon Borglum surveyed the Black Hills for rocky peaks of granite out of which to carve a national memorial. Gandhi was on a three week civil disobedience fast in India. A five-passenger Studebaker Standard Six sedan sold for $1,595. Silent film star Gloria Swanson was appearing in "Her Love Story" at the State Theater in Minneapolis. That evening, WLAG broadcast a two-hour program from the board room of the Washburn Crosby Company, as John Crosby announced that "application has been made to the bureau of navigation at Washington for a change of the station's call letters from WLAG to WCCO." The dance music continued until midnight. When party goers arose the following morning, WCCO Radio was born. On October 2, 1924, the Saint Paul Dispatch listed the first day's modest menu of programming on WCCO-417 meters, Saint Paul and Minneapolis, "The Gold Medal Station":

9:30 a.m.	Program for Day
9:40	Weather Report and Market Quotations
10:45	Home Service— Betty Crocker
11:30	Market Quotations
1:30 p.m.	Market Quotations and Weather Report
2:00	Home Service— Betty Crocker
4:00	Message Hour
4:30	Market Quotations
5:30	Children's Hour
6:00	Sports Hour
6:30	Dinner Concert
8:00	Lecture Hour, including Feed Talk
9:00	Weather Report
9:30	Musical Program

The rest of the decade was a swift passage. A tumbling of events one upon another at an ever faster pace. On March 4, 1925, WCCO began broadcasting from new studios on the 12th and 13th floors of the Nicollet Hotel, in downtown Minneapolis, opened a 5,000 watt transmitter on the site of an old chicken farm near Anoka, and that same evening broadcast President Coolidge's inaugural address.

THAT ONE PROGRAM made crystal sets obsolete in the Twin Cities. The station's signal, now 18 miles away, could be received only by tube radios in the Twin Cities.

In 1927, WCCO, one of the 21 original affiliates of the NBC Red Network, reported the triumphant return of aviator Charles Lindbergh to the Twin Cities, broadcast radio's first singing commercial (Christmas Eve, 1926, "Have you tried Wheaties?" written by Henry

Bellows and Earl Gammons) and became sole property of the Washburn Crosby Company after Twin Cities businessmen withdrew their financial support.

At precisely this time, events in New York were shaping a future that would change the course of WCCO. Twenty-six-year-old William Paley, working for his father's Congress Cigar Company, was astonished. Sales of his La Palina cigars doubled through the use of radio advertising on WCAU in Philadelphia and the Columbia Broadcasting System. Like Washburn Crosby and its flour, here was testimony to the commercial power of radio, or what former Commerce Secretary Hoover derisively called "advertising chatter." Paley moved to New York, bought CBS, and two years later, after Washburn Crosby had been gobbled up by General Mills, he bought one-third of WCCO for $150,000 with an option to buy the rest for $300,000 in three years. Paley bought his interest in WCCO after General Mills, so one story goes, wasn't

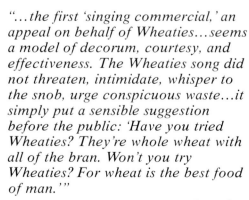

WCCO Radio's first general manager, Henry Bellows, above top: "If the broadcasters…are so stupid as to fail to look beyond the hope of a quick cash return, they may seriously injure and perhaps destroy their own business."

"…the first 'singing commercial,' an appeal on behalf of Wheaties…seems a model of decorum, courtesy, and effectiveness. The Wheaties song did not threaten, intimidate, whisper to the snob, urge conspicuous waste…it simply put a sensible suggestion before the public: 'Have you tried Wheaties? They're whole wheat with all of the bran. Won't you try Wheaties? For wheat is the best food of man.'"

James Gray
Business Without Boundaries
The Story of General Mills
1954

From WCCO Radio's Gold Medal Newsletter, 1925

"…peremptory notice was served on WCCO one night at nine o'clock, to broadcast for a man who did not come home to dinner. From the tone of the feminine voice, this disappearance was entirely unaccountable… needless to say, the broadcast was not made…"

———

"There is no getting away from the radio. In one coal mine in Illinois, the miners blithely blast to the airy strains broadcast from The Gold Medal Station."

———

"Radio stations are supposed to know everything. For instance, during the recent Minnesota State Fair, a woman called at the Gold Medal Station headquarters and asked where was the best place to get a shingle bob."

———

"The limit for mid-day reception on my five-tube tregodine set—Today woman's voices—markets, grains, stocks, bonds—perfectly clear, signing off at 10-39 1/4, Gold Medal Station, WCCO. This is about 750 miles, as the crow flies. Bright sunshine day, litle (sic) cool. Your station easy to get at night, but had no idea could get it at mid-day."

Yours truly,
B.L. Kemp
Adamsville, Tennessee

———

"The Gold Medal Station is now operating on what is probably the heaviest broadcasting schedule in the United States, and perhaps in the world, with an average of ten and one-half hours of actual transmission each day, seven days a week."

———

"…I am a Minnesotan…your voice came to me so clear and plain last evening, while sitting in my little home here in the foothills of the Sierras…"

J.T. Blackburn
Paradise, Butte County, California

It was plain and simple, broadcasting in the 1920's, but it transfixed listeners throughout the Northwest. Above, a WCCO Radio studio at the Nicollet Hotel in all its austere decor, and the broadcast booth for early University of Minnesota football play-by-play from Memorial Stadium, Minneapolis. WCCO Radio has covered every Minnesota Gopher football game, home and away, for 60 years.

able to give the station away to either the City of Minneapolis or the City of Saint Paul. General Mills, in desperation, even offered to cover expenses for the first year. WCCO surrendered its NBC affiliation when it chose to carry its broadcast of the Minneapolis Symphony sponsored by Northwestern National Bank, rather than clear that same Sunday evening time for an NBC broadcast of the Chicago Symphony sponsored by Standard Oil. NBC went to KSTP, CBS to WCCO.

In August, 1929, Wilbur Foshay's spectacular 32-story tower was dedicated in downtown Minneapolis, an extravaganza featuring John Philip Sousa that cost $116,000. Two months later, the stock market collapsed. WCCO and the Northwest were headed for the most violent economic upheaval of the century. "The Big Bull Market had been more than the climax of a business cycle," wrote Frederick Lewis Allen in *Only Yesterday,* "it had been the climax of a cycle in mass thinking and mass emotion. There was hardly a man or woman in the country whose attitude toward life had not been affected by it in some degree and was not now affected by the sudden and brutal shattering of hope."

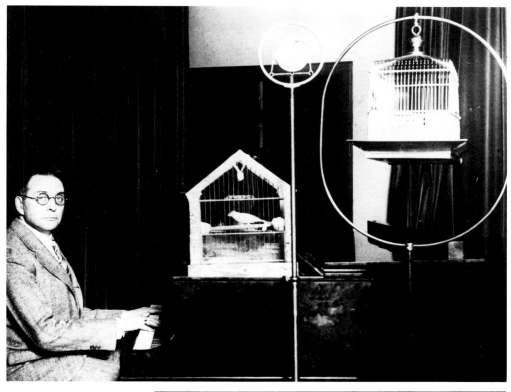

*Varied amusements: left,
some early WCCO Radio
programming was for the birds;
below, Irish tenor Jerry Harrington,
pianist Irene Harris, announcer Fred
Laws; one of the early WCCO Radio
booths at the Minnesota State Fair,
circa 1925.*

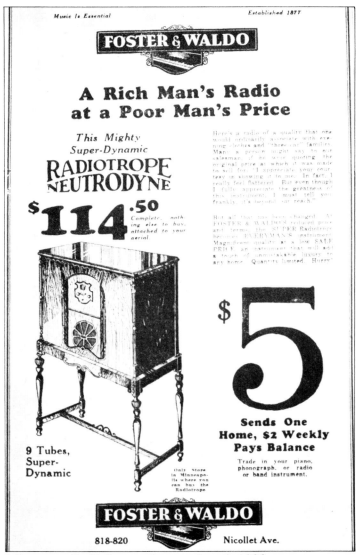
Minneapolis Tribune, September 6, 1929.

19

THE

30's

MINNEAPOLIS, MINNESOTA

Dear Ed,

Marge just put the kids to bed. I'm up late again looking through the want ads for jobs. Believe me, there's not much out there. I stood in line again today at an employment agency for about four hours and froze. For the first time in my life, I've got to admit I'm scared. If Marge didn't have that part-time stenographer job, I don't know how we'd buy food and keep up the house payments. Our savings are gone. We've borrowed as much as we can against the life insurance. The gas bill came today. Marge has been putting in 18-hour days. This has been going on for a year next month. Tim is eight years old now and won't be able to have new shoes. We cut out cardboard to cover the holes in the soles. Marge gets by making dresses from drapery, and she's sewn patches over the worn elbows on my only business suit. I'm not complaining. Almost everybody else on the block is in the same fix. Things could be worse. I saw some people rummaging through one of the garbage cans in our alley this afternoon. Doesn't seem possible we played together as brothers in that same alley 15 years ago. Those were good times.

Marge and I sat in the living room last night and listened to Governor Olson on WCCO. He really gave the local press hell for criticizing him for the way he tried to settle that strike down at the Hormel plant in Austin. Get this. The paper quotes him this morning saying, "These blood-thirsty swivel-chair warriors whose only knowledge of life is gained through traveling from their homes to the sanctuary of their editorial rooms, thence to their exclusive clubs, and then back home...They do not know that it needs but one spark to start a veritable conflagration in this nation, and in their supreme egotism I presume they do not care."

Speaking of WCCO, radio's about the only entertainment we can afford these days. Don't have 20 cents for the movies. So we stay at home most nights and listen to WCCO. Marge likes that young crooner, Bing Crosby, who I could care less for. I like the Boswell Sisters and Ben Bernie ("Yowsah! yowsah! yowsah!"). The only newspaper column I read is Cedric Adams in the Minneapolis Shopping News handout. He should be in radio. Papers are filled with so much bad news, which we get enough of without reading the papers. Radio's good for the spirits.

Don't know how the economy is out East where you are. Here it's a mess. Unemployment is 20 per cent in the Twin Cities, 70 per cent on the Iron Range. WCCO says Minnesota had about 1,500 banks in 1921, and about 500 of them had closed by three years ago. Another 100 banks went under in 1931. This new Northwest Banking Corp. is helping some. They've got controlling interest now in close to 130 banks. Not everyone's suffering. Honeywell's laid off a lot of employees, but General Mills and Dayton's don't seem to be hurting. It's bad on the farms. Remember, when we were growing up, wheat sold for about $3.00 a bushel? Now it's 60 cents in Minneapolis. This new Farmers' Holiday Association is holding back crops til the farmers get at least cost of production. I think they're on the right track.

21

Even with that, depends where you live. Only about three per cent of the people in Goodhue County just south of here depend on federal relief. But in Big Stone County, out near the Dakota border, it's about 60 per cent, because of the drought and one-crop farms. Some people say there could be as many as 20,000 unemployed in Minneapolis, (including yours truly). That's out of a total population of 465,000. This Methodist minister, George Mecklenburg, has done a lot of good with his Organized Unemployment, Inc....issuing scrip for barter as payment for labor. But it's not enough.

I don't know if you voted for FDR, Ed, but I did. Say what you want about his Harvard accent and his arrogance, at least he's not sitting on his hands like Hoover. This new Federal Emergency Relief Act is going to provide a lot of jobs here in Minnesota, and the Agricultural Adjustment Administration is going to give farmers a break. Same with the CCC for young people. We've got to do something to reduce the farm surpluses. The only way out now seems to be controlling crop acreage and giving farmers those benefit checks. We listened to FDR on WCCO a few weeks back, one of his so-called "fireside chats." I got the feeling he wasn't up on a stage but talking to Marge and me right in our home. He and Governor Olson have one thing in common, they both know how to use radio. Speaking of Olson, I'm worried about what might happen if

this labor-management thing in Minneapolis gets any worse. The management organization, which is called the Citizens Alliance, is giving us a reputation as an anti-union town, and I don't know how long the unions are going to stand for it, especially the truckers. All you need is a spark like Olson said. I'm worried there could be bloodshed.

Ed, the real reason for this letter is to ask you a big favor. Marge and I would like to know if you could lend us $200 to get us through the winter. We promise to pay you back as soon as we can. It's not easy to ask for a loan, especially from my kid brother, but when you're trying to support a family of five on $15 a week, nothing is beneath your pride. You know I'm no freeloader. I wouldn't think of taking a hand-out from anyone. This would just be a straight loan between brothers. Marge and I would honor it with our word. We aren't planning any sort of Christmas this year, at least not the Santa Claus kind. We'd use the money just to pay the bills. I'll get a job soon (maybe). Some day I hope I can help you. Well, have to go. Marge wants to listen to Bing Crosby on WCCO. Maybe better times are just around the corner—personally, I doubt it.

*Love from Marge and the kids
and Bob*

A farm family in the Depression, Minnesota, circa 1932.

1930-1939

Sixty Years Strong

"*I should say the broadcasts from WCCO help. Some of them (our customers) do not even ask for a demonstration (of Aladdin lamps,) just tell us to wrap it up. WCCO is used more than any other station.*"

W.E. Johnig
Britton, South Dakota

Spring, 1932

H E WAS A BALDING newspaperman with a wisp of a mustache. With his friendly, moon-shaped face, perpetual pipesmoke and three-piece suits, he could have passed for a character actor in a Frank Capra movie. He knew almost nothing about radio when he came to WCCO in the late 1920's. Washburn Crosby wanted him to handle publicity for its radio station so dutifully he obeyed. In a matter of months, he transferred his faith and allegiance from a medium he could see and feel to one that was invisible.

It takes talent to find talent. Earl Gammons found it in the 1930's

WCCO Radio's two new 300-foot towers under construction, near Anoka, 1932...

for WCCO Radio. He did it without audition tapes, "head hunters" and ratings. He used trial and error and instinct. Radio still had not saturated the countryside. Fully one-third of the households in the Twin Cities did not have radio in 1932. Much of the economy was in a desperate tailspin. Hunger marchers descended on Washington D.C. A moratorium had been declared on foreclosures on first mortgages, a life line for families in their homes. FDR spoke of the "forgotten man at the bottom of the economic pyramid" and closed the nation's banks for four days to stop a panic. WCCO Radio was a handsome island of prosperity in the midst of this turbulence. One of its 1932 sales pitches proclaimed, perhaps a bit naively, "You'll find no hectic ups and downs in the charted incomes of Northwest families. They have that typical steadiness of an agricultural background—of an agriculture that is widely diversified—of an industry built mainly on the needs of this diversified farm economy. The Northwest family is your 'middle-western' type—solid, home-building, thrifty, ambitious for the modern standards of life." *If* you had a job.

There were more than enough jobs in radio. WCCO, and stations like it, had become so popular that they helped depress the sale of phonographs and sheet music, pianos and violins, theater tickets and newspaper advertising. They even shortened the average life of a popular song from two years to six to eight weeks. Commercial networks, what someone called mere "tissue of contracts," nonetheless created national loyalty to national radio cele-

"I was instructed…to go up and help with the publicity on a new venture called a radio station. I was confident that the officers of Washburn-Crosby responsible for this…must have lost their minds. And after I had been on the job for about three months I was sure I had lost mine."

Earl Gammons
General Manager, WCCO Radio
1931-1942

…and completed.

The 1930's — the genesis of personality radio at WCCO: Al Harding, Bob Campbell, Ed Abbott, Roy Brant, Clellan Card, Eddie Gallaher, and Charlie Ross. Learning to touch a listener with a warm, human style. Above: A view from the top of the "stick" that made it possible, WCCO's antenna near Anoka, 1939, the tallest structure in Minnesota at the time, 654 feet.

brities and national product brands. By 1935, William Paley had built CBS into the network with the most stations (97) using a quasi-monopolistic lever: offering an entire sustaining (non-sponsored) schedule free to affiliates, for an option on any part of an affiliate's schedule for sponsored shows. In effect, local stations such as WCCO, as Erik Barnouw wrote, ceded control of a sizeable portion of their schedules to an absentee landlord. About three-fourths of an average WCCO broadcast day originated from Columbia in New York. Networks hired entertainers, many of them former hoofers, vaudevillians and dance hall comics. Gammons looked for entertainers too, but also sought personalities who could touch a listener with a warm, human, neighborly style. Enter-

tainers had one dimension. Personalities, if they were good, had three. But they were few, and often resigned to nothing more than introducing the endless parade of musicians who passed before the radio microphone. The Northwest, with its German-Scandinavian heritage, was a land of musicians: church choirs, symphony orchestras, glee clubs, choral groups, touring bands. Gammons and Al Sheehan, the head of the station's "artists' bureau," turned WCCO Radio into a virtual conservatory of live, popular music in the 1930's. It seemed as if most of the sound that bounced its merry way across the nation during the decade from the new 50,000 watt transmitter in Anoka was music: Eddie Dunstedter (thumping away on the giant Wurlitzer organ from studios at the Nicollet Hotel, the

largest pipe organ ever built, so WCCO claimed, by any radio station), pianists Ramona Gerhard and Toby Prin, Eddie Fortier, Rollie Altmeyer, Andy Kenney and his band, Jack Malerich and his "Singing Strings," band leader Wally Olson, tenor Walter Mallory, Jerry Harrington ("The Little Irish Tenor"), Harry Habata and his accordian, blues singer Jerry Gardner, banjo player Bruce Patterson, "The Red River Valley Gang," harmonica players Tom

Clellan Card, Eddie Gallaher on WCCO Radio, November, 1939, "The Kitchen Quiz": "A virtual conservatory of live, popular music..."

and Eddie Plehal, and singers Hal and Ernie Garven and Dick Link.

Each developed a loyal, and in some cases, large following. They cherished what was perhaps the only relatively secure day job for musicians in the market. But their days on radio were numbered and though they charmed listeners they were not the vital seed which eventually made WCCO Radio distinctive. Under Gammons, personalities gradually became family for thousands of households in the Northwest: Cedric Adams, Halsey Hall, Clellan Card and Larry Haeg Sr., among others. One could marvel at the sound of the hulking Wurlitzer, but it was not a flesh and blood companion.

Gammons had the good fortune to inherit a solid base for all this, prepared by one just as unlikely to manage a radio station: Harvard Ph.D. Henry Bellows, a rhetoric professor from the University of Minnesota who had edited a literary magazine and dabbled in poetry. He believed in free enterprise, to a point. "If the broadcasters…are so stupid as to fail to look beyond the hope of a quick cash return," he wrote in 1932, after service on the Federal Radio Commission, "they may seriously injure and perhaps destroy their own business." It was Bellows during his tenure on the commission in the early 1930's who may have done the station

the biggest favor—perhaps pulling the wires that gave WCCO its favorable AM dial position and 50,000 watts clear channel. Bellows and Gammons became CBS vice presidents. It was Gammons who fashioned personality radio and remote broadcasts on WCCO, an imprint that survives today.

In 1931, he discovered the 29-year-old son of a bank cashier from Magnolia, Minnesota, who was making something of a name for himself as a columnist for the Minneapolis Shopping News. He paid him $3.50 for a small role in the drama, "The Curtains Part." No recording was made, but it is

"Maybe this is what radio was all about…ultimately optimistic, undeniably innocent by today's standards" Clockwise: Toby Prin and the WCCO Radio orchestra, celebrity interviewer Florence *Lehmann of "Ladies First," newscaster Eddie Gallaher, Bruce Patterson on banjo, pianist Ramona Gerhard, Teena and Tim, and the crowds that waited in line for the magic of live radio.*

Live music in the night: the Johnny Gilbert orchestra from the Hotel Lowry in Saint Paul on WCCO Radio, circa 1939.

said that during that broadcast on WCCO, or one shortly thereafter, Cedric Adams first chose to violate a sacred canon of early radio. During that live drama, something in the deadly script struck him as terribly funny.

He laughed.

A spontaneous, mirthful, naughty, and unfortunately, untimely, laugh. "We finally figured there wasn't much of a future for him," said Gammons years later, "so we dropped him." The Adams experiment could have ended there, save a chance conversation Gammons had with the *Minneapolis Star's* Basil "Stuffy" Walters, who was looking for someone to do a column for the *Star* and, perhaps,

read newscasts on WCCO Radio. Adams began reading the 10:00 p.m. news on WCCO in September, 1934, the year of the Dust Bowl, the year of the first national football championship under Bernie Bierman at the University of Minnesota, the year Hitler became president of the Reich and made all members of the German armed forces take an absolute oath of obedience to the Fuhrer, the year Ronald "Dutch" Reagan joined WHO in Des Moines.

Cedric Adams was a new breed. He was not strictly an entertainer or performer, not a comedian or master of ceremonies, nor did he have a journalist's sense of news.

He was, rather, with his warm, resonant, textured voice, and roots in the Minnesota countryside, a man who listened to and liked people, who knew well how to make them like him.

FOR 27 YEARS HE WAS perhaps the most widely known, highest paid radio personality at any station in the United States. He wore the finest suits, expensive colognes, yet seemed in his element in a hardware store in Owatonna, on a farm in Redwood Falls, or in a board of directors room of a Twin Cities savings and loan. If it was an act, it was a good one, a deception of great proportions.

There was more to WCCO in the 1930's than Cedric Adams. He would not reach the height of his popularity until the 1940's and 1950's. There was other home grown talent, the dentist's son from Minneapolis, Clellan Card, with his corny repertoire of "Birdie with the Yellow Bill" jokes and his outlandish Scandinavian dialect. There was Halsey Hall, son of a Shakespearian actress, who turned down a network offer and joined WCCO to broadcast play-by-play for the Minneapolis Millers at Nicollet Park. There was a soap opera-comedy with Swedish dialect, "Teena and Tim," which eventually went to the network and bombed there in the 1940's. "It may have been" wrote John Dunning in his encyclopedia of old time radio, "one of the reasons radio died." The mistake, perhaps, was trying to transplant an indigenous show to a national stage. Cedric, Halsey, Clellan, Teena and Tim, "The Red River Valley Gang" were not really meant for New York or Los Angeles. It was like trying to grow corn in mid-town Manhattan.

As the networks sometimes proved, though, the reverse could work. The soap opera did that. *The Romance of Helen Trent* premiered on the network and WCCO October 30, 1933. "Time now for the Romance of Helen Trent," said narrator Fielden Farrington 7,222 times for 27 years on WCCO, "the real-life drama of Helen Trent, who— when life mocks her, breaks her hopes, dashes her against the rocks of despair—fights back bravely, successfully, to prove what so many women long to prove in their own lives; that because a woman is 35, and more, romance in life need not be over, that the romance of youth can extend into middle life, and even

From "The Ghost Walks Again," an adventure of "The Shadow" starring Lamont Cranston on CBS and WCCO Radio:

EDWARD: In the days of the Puritans they had a very satisfactory method for dealing with meddlers...they branded them upon the forehead...

MARGO: No...no...

EDWARD: Soon, young lady, soon you shall feel the searing agony of that brand biting into your flesh.

MARGO: You're mad...you're mad!

EDWARD: (laughing) You won't feel the pain too long...no...you see, after you are branded I have another treat for you...the press...the torture press!

MARGO: You let me out of here!

EDWARD: The branding iron is glowing now...it is ready to use!

MARGO: You can't do this...please!

EDWARD: (laughing) Prepare yourself...prepare yourself, Miss Lane...I have the iron ready now...

MARGO: Keep it away from me...(screams) Keep it away!

SHADOW: Drop that iron, Mr. Darrow!

EDWARD: Who was that?

SHADOW: Release that girl...

EDWARD: No...no! Let go of my arm! Let me finish my work!

(iron drops to floor)

SHADOW: Then you know too that I am here to put an end to your career of torture and murder, Mr. Darrow!

beyond..." Helen Trent, and Ma Perkins, the back porch conscience of Rushville Center, sponsored by Oxydol, survived on WCCO Radio until 1960.

On Thursday, April 7, 1938, three weeks after Hitler's invasion of Austria and the premiere of the *CBS World News Roundup,* WCCO moved from its cluttered quarters at the Nicollet Hotel to the nondescript Elks Club building at 625 Second Avenue South. CBS architects, nonetheless, liked the building with its high ceilings and fourth floor auditorium. The CBS design, almost identical to other Paley projects in Chicago, Saint Louis and Boston, included features that have never been surpassed in acoustical quality. It had floating studios (the floor, walls and ceiling of each of the six studios were separated from the rest of the structure). The entrance to each studio had a short hallway and two heavy, "sound lock" doors. Sloping glass partitions between studio and control room prevented glare and reflection. In deference to sponsors, each studio had a client audition room. The musicians, still the station's premier talent, had their own lounge. The elegant circular lobby, in Columbia blue and satin wood with indirect lighting, had it survived the renovation of the 1950's, would have affectionately been called "art deco."

Minneapolis Tribune sports columnist Charlie Johnson, right, with University of Minnesota head football coach Bernie Bierman on WCCO Radio in 1934, the year the Gophers won their first national title.

This scarcely illuminates the most important question: what did WCCO sound like day in and day out in the 1930's? The embarrassing truth is we do not know for sure. It was before the whir of audio tape, before the routine daily use of electronic transcription, before any self-appointed archivist saved anything except random programs of special interest. Even recollections of those who were there are selective and distorted. One knows, easily enough, what the daily program schedule was—but it is the *sound* of the station from sunrise to sunset that now is impossible to retrieve. It probably fit the pace and flow of Midwestern life: comfortable, conservative, relaxed, warm, amiable. It doubtless reflected the taste and values of most of its white, middle class listeners. A woman's place was in the home. A man's place was in the office. Most authority unquestioned. The music live. News stolen from newspapers. The soap operas, the dramatized news, were continuing morality plays. "Maybe this is what radio was all about," wrote John Dunning, "ultimately optimistic, undeniably innocent

by today's standards, old-time radio conveyed noble myths: crime did not pay, goodness would always be rewarded, and evil would not go unpunished." Far beyond the farmfields and silos of Minnesota, an evil of frightening dimensions was gathering force in Europe. It would send a ripple of fear through America and change the sound of radio in the 1940's.

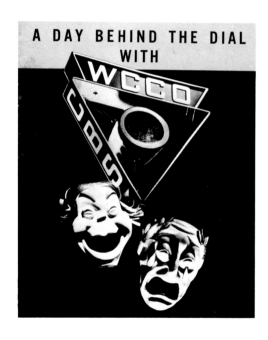

A DAY BEHIND THE DIAL WITH

THE 40's

ST. PAUL, MINNESOTA

Looking back at the war years for me is like trying to see through a fogged-up window. It's hard to remember exactly what was going through my head those years without Tom. Things happened so fast. You never knew what was coming. The uncertainty made you jumpy. You'd look down and see your hand shaking your coffee cup. A feeling of nausea in your stomach. Just a vague, uneasy sense of dread that you couldn't put into words. Then just the opposite, there are other things I remember very vividly. Right down to the color of a dress or some insignificant detail like some casual remark that stuck with me. Like remembering exactly where I was (in the basement doing laundry) the first time I heard "Don't Sit Under the Apple Tree with Anyone Else But Me" on WCCO. Dumb, right?

It is absolutely branded into my memory that Sunday of the Pearl Harbor attack. Tom and I had celebrated our third anniversary the week before. He had a good job with an engineering firm. We had bought a two bedroom house on Randolph Avenue in Saint Paul. He was 26. I was 23, our oldest son, Tommy, Junior, was one year old. He's married now, living in Roseville, with a wife and four children. Anne was on the way. We had just gotten back from noon Mass at the Cathedral and were reading the paper in the living room, listening to the Longines Symphonette on WCCO. I remember the clock on the mantle. It was 2:25. The bulletin came on, John Daly of CBS. I remember he was so shook he mis-pronounced the Hawaiian Island of Oahu. The bulletin only lasted about a minute.

Then they went back to the symphony. I'll never forget the look on Tom's face. First it was just blank. Then anger. He threw the sports section down and whispered one word, "bastards." His face went white.

He enlisted the next week, did basic in Texas and eight months later he was in the Pacific. I didn't hear his voice for three years. That sounds like a long time. God, it was. But life had to go on. If you let it get to you, you'd go crazy. So you kept busy, just to keep your mind off it. And it wasn't as if you were the only one. The war touched everyone on Randolph, every one in Saint Paul. Everyone had their own way of dealing with it. Self-pity was simply admitting you weren't strong enough to take it, and I didn't want that. So all of us felt united, together, helping each other get through it. I did volunteer work for the Red Cross, taking the streetcar downtown to the Saint Paul Union depot where we handed out sandwiches, doughnuts and coffee and Cokes to soldiers. Saint Paul was sort of a natural stopping point for troop transport trains between Chicago and the West Coast.

One of the things that didn't make sense was that for the first time in several years, we had plenty of money, but nowhere to spend it. The war really pumped up the economy but nice things were hard to get. People stood in line to buy meat, sometimes paying $1.25 a pound for boneless ham. Pork chops were 38 cents a pound. We punched oleo up in a bag to make it look like butter, because butter was really scarce.

The word got out once that a store near The

College of St. Catherine had butter. There was a line of twenty people there within a couple of hours. There were stamps for rationing gasoline, meat and sugar. I remember one sign in a restaurant on Wabasha, "Use a little sugar and stir like hell. We don't mind the noise." Actually, I never stood in line for a thing. If Tom could go without, so could we. It was hard to indulge in personal pleasures. Even if I wanted to go out I couldn't. Nightclubs and downtown restaurants were always crowded, and the government put a 20 percent tax increase on liquor. Minneapolis was almost out of liquor once. Some people were paying $12 a pint for cheap bourbon. So, we spent a lot of time at home. I planted a Victory Garden and did a lot of vegetable canning. If you did want to go grocery shopping, there were some big, new stores, called supermarkets. There were new appliances too. We didn't buy some of them til after the war: automatic toasters, dishwashers, electric coffeemakers, ice cube makers, Revere ware and eight mm movie cameras. Actually, it was kind of exhilarating to know you could get by on less. Growing up in the Depression, that wasn't hard for us. They needed nylon for parachutes, so I didn't buy nylons. Some women did, for $5 a pair, on the black market. You weren't supposed to travel unless it was absolutely necessary. Signs at gasoline stations said, "Is This Trip Necessary?" The OPA actually stopped some people in their cars. Pleasure driving just wasn't done much. The government ordered car manufacturing stopped. I kept our '35 Studebaker running til Tom got back. Once I had to pay $46 for a pair of old tires as bald as Uncle Frank. Right after Pearl Harbor there was some hoarding of coffee, clothing and such, but mostly people shared. Some of the government's orders were stupid: like saying men's suits couldn't have an extra pair of trousers, to save wool. Or making dresses without zippers and pleats. It was a different world for women. I remember they called 1943 "maid's year off." We really did keep the economy going. There weren't any day care centers in those days, and we got a fraction of the pay men got for the same jobs. Just the same, millions of women like myself entered the work force for the first time. I got a job at a defense plant. For the first time since we were married, we had a second income.

You want me to write about radio in those days. Well, what can I say, it was a way of life. I remember every night during the war when H.V. Kaltenborn came on. He didn't just talk about the misery and the suffering and the brutality of war, he made you feel it with his voice, as I recall a very caring, sensitive voice. I remember even before Pearl Harbor, Tom and I would sit in the living room and listen to Edward R. Murrow of CBS on WCCO during the Battle of Britain. You felt as if we were up there on the rooftop with him. One night I happened to have a pencil in my hand. I wrote down what he said and saved it. "The searchlights straightaway, miles in front of me, are still scratching the sky. There's a three-quarter moon riding high. There was one burst of shellfire almost straight in the Little Dipper." I remember one day in September, 1943, when Kate Smith, the singer, was on WCCO and Columbia something like 65 times from eight in the morning to two a.m. the next day for War Bond Day. She raised $39 million worth of bonds. All day long, WCCO was telling how you could become an air raid warden, how to learn first aid, donate scrap, give blood. The music was mostly patriotic songs from World War I. They weren't allowed to play one called "Der Fuhrer's Face" (because it said what should be done with Hitler's face.) Then there were the casualty lists on radio. Every day a new list, sometimes on and on with unfamiliar names until you heard the name of a guy killed in the Pacific or in North Africa, a guy you used to go to high school with. Not just a name any more but an awful waste. There were plenty of live radio reports from Europe during the war, but not much that I can recall from the Pacific where Tom was. Just the same, I remember following the Battle of Okinawa on WCCO with a map at the kitchen table. Bataan. Corrigidor. Midway. Iwo Jima, Wake. I'd say to myself, "Tom is there." I found in a book this afternoon the words that Archibald MacLeish had read on his show on Columbia called "This is War!": "What we say tonite has to do with blood and bone and with anger, and with a big job in the making. Laughter can wait, soft music can have the evening off. No one is invited to sit down and take it easy…." We girls did go out sometimes, just for escape. My favorite movie in 1943 was Bing Crosby and Barry Fitzgerald in "Going My Way." Once I even flouted the rules to let Tom know I hadn't lost my sense of humor. I mixed a batch of martinis and had a friend of mine at the local canning company put it in a sealed orange juice can. It got past customs and Tom had a party with his buddies somewhere in the Pacific. Near the end of the war, there were rumors that even I thought were just ridiculous. Our neighbor, Sarah, told me she had heard that the Japanese were going to attack the Panama Canal and that their bombers would fly from Tokyo, refuel at the Aleutians via Alaska and bomb the Twin Cities on their way. In 1942 it would have made me sick to my stomach but now, in 1944, I had to laugh. Sarah didn't think it was so funny.

I cried on V-E Day. I cried on V-J Day. I cried the morning the phone rang and heard Tom's distant voice for the first time in three years. He was in San Francisco and would be home in two days. This may sound terribly sappy, like some Hollywood B movie, but it really did happen this way. We waited for Tom's plane to come in at Wold Chamberlain air field. I saw him come out of the plane but I couldn't tell for sure if it was him because he looked so thin. Little Tommy knew him only from photos and he had only seen pictures of Anne, had never held her. When he was about 20 yards from us, in his uniform and carrying his duffle bag, little Tommy yelled out "There's Daddy!" The next few months and years were not easy. Distance had strained our marriage. We needed professional counseling. But somehow we survived and grew. It was a lot like that movie they made later, "The Best Years of Our Lives."

One morning a few weeks later, Tom was in the kitchen listening to the radio, washing dishes and just said to no one in particular, "Good to hear Cedric again."

World War II, The Saint Paul Union Depot, 1942.

1940-1949

Sixty Years Strong

"*If I ever stop knowing people and what they think, I'm through.*"

Cedric Adams

IT WAS A COMMONPLACE room of unadorned Midwestern plainness, unaffected as a farm kitchen. It was on the fourth floor of the WCCO Radio building, about the size of a small town high school gymnasium, trimmed in cream and Columbia blue. It had a hardwood floor, rows of folding metal chairs to seat about 700 people, a small stage that held, at most, a 20-piece orchestra, and off stage right, a booth for engineer and producer with the size and look of an icehouse with windows on two sides. From this unpretentious setting, day and night, in all seasons, music, laughter, applause and the human voice were sparked into electromagnetic

energy and tossed through the air to millions of delighted listeners in their homes. It was, insist those who heard it, some of the best live radio ever. Or perhaps, a nostalgic haze only makes it seem so now.

One can still listen today, on scratchy disc or muffled tape, to the sounds that came from this room. But the room is gone. It disappeared in a barely-noted renovation sometime in the late 1950's, after such radio had mostly gone the way of the crystal set

and Victrola. In its prime, this room vibrated with the essence of WCCO Radio. Almost any given day or night one could walk into it and become a joyful part of something that went bouncing far beyond its four drab walls, through the region in the day, the nation at night. The tickets were free, the entertainment (like the twice a day vaudevilles of an earlier generation) was happily predictable: the Red River Valley Gang or Jack Malerich and his Orchestra, rotund (they used that

word a lot those days) Cedric Adams' *Stairway to Stardom* or genial (that word too) Bob DeHaven and the *Murphy Barn Dance.*

For the chance to see Adams or DeHaven and tap your feet to the music, the only price you paid was having to listen to commercials for Taystee Bread, Cargill Feeds or Phillips Oil. In an odd way, they were entertainment too. Columbia's pin-striped executives in New York may have thought it hokey, but they did not laugh at the profit margin. At one point during the 1940's, on Friday nights, this auditorium was the

Bob DeHaven, Clellan Card, hosts for "The Quiz of the Twin Cities."

39

site of five consecutive studio audience shows, *all* five individually sponsored.

THERE WAS NO SECRET to its success. The 50,000-watt-clear-channel giant created the star system, and the stars worked hard to cultivate a mass audience with warmth, friendliness, old jokes and live music. The housewives in cloth coats, farmers in Sunday best, considered Adams, Card and DeHaven and all the rest, part of the family. "They knew who I was and they came to have a good time," said DeHaven years later, recalling the audience warm-up before the show, "I'd say, 'Now let's try some applause.' And invariably, it was scattered. I'd say, 'I can't put *that* on the air, you gotta make more noise

than that. Now try it again.' And woooosh, the applause would just *roll* up on stage. We did have fun. We *did* have fun."

Before television, before "record shows," before disc jockeys, this was, if there ever was such a thing, the golden age of local radio. "There was writing going on," said DeHaven, "and rehearsing and producing and arranging music and ideas flying around and talent flying around. It wasn't the epitome of entertainment but it was damn good radio."

Lines for free tickets grew longer. Ratings increased. The best live shows, instead of waiting for listeners to come to them, went on the road. Adams did his *Saturday Night Radio Party* from Excelsior Amusement Park during the summer, took

Stairway to Stardom to hundreds of towns in the Northwest. They were greeted with a frenzy of innocent enthusiasm. By the end of the decade, Adams alone was making more than 150 personal appearances a year, many on weekends with talent from *Stairway,* known on the road as *Cedric Adams' Open House,* sponsored by Northern States Power Company. It was, in hindsight, a corny array of talent but it fit the times perfectly, playing to standing room only at dingy armories all over the countryside. At one time, the troupe included an eight-year-old girl who yodeled, two baton twirlers, an accordian player, a magician, a comedy team, three singing sisters, and the Queen of the Minneapolis Aquatennial.

At its peak, the group was on the road 49 weekends a year, 12 to 18 hours each trip, about 300 miles

each performance, 15,000 miles a year, surviving snowstorms, flat tires, rickety bridges and a near-fatal accident outside Annandale at night on ice. On stage, the older the joke, the older the routine, the more certain the laughter. Sometimes, two local men would be coaxed from the audience to wear white union suits and inflate balloons in the bellies of each others' suits with air pumps. Women from the audience giggled their way on stage to dress like men, and vice versa. Or, said Cedric, in town after town, did

An informal family portrait, left, as General Manager Earl Gammons departs for CBS in 1942; the mid-1940's Gopher football broadcast team, right, Bill Bloedel, Babe Levoir, Halsey Hall and Paul Wann; and below, old jokes and doughnuts: Hale Byers and Clellan Card in the early morning.

The tickets free, the entertainment happily predictable. Top right, the Cedric Adams "Stairway to Stardom" show; right, on the road with the Murphy Seed Barn Dance in Fergus Falls; and bottom, the Doughboy Country Journal, at table, Gordon Eaton and Larry Haeg. Standing: Willie Peterson (at piano), Mary Davies, Tony Grise, Irv Wickner, Biddy Bastien, (accordionist unidentified), Frankie Roberts, Ernie Garvin, Burt Hanson, Hal Garvin and Dick Link.

you hear about the lady who went into the drug store to get some powder? She told the clerk what she wanted and the clerk said, "Please walk this way." "If I could walk that way," she said, "I wouldn't need the powder." Or, "All you ladies who are here with your husbands, raise your right hand. Oh, that's fine. Now, all you men who are here with your wives, raise your hands. That's good. But I see some of you didn't raise your hands. Some of you guys must be here with some strange dames." After the show, Cedric wrote, "I get out at the door like a preacher with his congregation, shaking hands. People tell me what they think. If I ever stop knowing people and what they think, I'm through." Then, to a local restaurant for a late supper with the troupe. Just as Cedric's steak arrived, a farmer

invariably would introduce himself. Cedric would set his steak aside and ask, in a tone of really wanting to know, "How many cows are you milking?"

This simple, direct, personal appeal created product loyalty and enormous profits. Adams' 12:30 p.m. newscast, it was said, had the largest Hooper rating of any local radio show in the nation. Myth began to mingle with fact. Was it true that a farmer deposited $8,000 with a savings and loan in the Twin Cities, then withdrew it a few hours later, saying he really wanted to open an account at "the place Cedric talks about on WCCO?" (Twin City Federal). Was it true that another listener had sent him a check for $10,000 to open an account for him at TCF? Who can say it could not have happened? In 1949, Cedric and WCCO alone raised an estimated $175,000, called "the largest amount ever collected by any single station in the country in the history of the March of Dimes" up to that time. During World War II, using the influence of WCCO and his daily column in the *Minneapolis Star,* close to 23,000 people claimed they went on diets at his behest, losing an average of almost seven pounds each. Adams himself took the extraordinary step of confessing on the air during one nightly newscast (sponsored by Taystee Bread) that he had been guilty of over-indulging in liquor. He promised to go on the wagon. His listeners admired his honesty but the abstemious pledge didn't last.

By 1948, the station claimed an independent diary survey had WCCO the favorite 19-1 among listeners in 128 counties. Nationwide, it was part of an industry with an embarrassment of wealth. From 1942-1944, radio advertising budgets increased from $195,000,000 to $390,000,000. In 1943, radio passed newspapers as a national advertising medium, increasing its share of national advertising dollars from 12 per cent in 1941, to 18 per cent in 1945. Even the government helped. During World War II, it slapped a 90 per cent excess profits tax on industry to discourage profiteering in war contracts, but allowed excess profits used in *advertising* taxable at normal rates. Thus, until 1945, sponsors could buy a dollar's worth of advertising on WCCO and other stations, in effect, for ten cents. Competition increased. WCCO was one of 543 commercial AM stations in the United States in 1940, one of 919 in 1945, one of 2,062 in 1950.

FOR ALL THEIR NATURAL charm, local variety shows were still outnumbered in the Forties by proliferating soap operas from Columbia in New York. It was, in fact, possible to sit down and listen to WCCO on a given day—June 16, 1944—at 8:45 a.m. and listen to an almost uninterrupted cascade of eleven 15-minute soap operas and three 15-minute serials until almost 2:00 p.m. The torrent

of characters and plots overwhelmed the ear and the heart: *Judy and Jane* (beautiful housewife and wise-cracking friend), *Valiant Lady* (soft-spoken heroine lives a quiet life in a "gossipy little town"), *Light of the World* (contemporary adaptation of Old Testament stories), *The Open Door* (the lives and loves of the dean of a university), *Bachelor's Children* (the life of Dr. Bob Graham whose "promise to his dying sergeant in the Great War brought him two nearly grown girls to raise"—one of whom he marries), *Second Husband, Bright Horizon, Big Sister* (the story of Ruth Evans "as she guides her younger sister and brother through the trials of life"), *The Romance of Helen Trent, Our Gal Sunday* ("can this girl from a mining town in the West find

Below, Ed Viehman describes the 1946 Minneapolis Aquatennial: right, Clellan Card, one of the top talents at WCCO Radio in the 1940's, during "Freshman Week" at the University of Minnesota, and below right, in his "birdie with the yellow bill" attire.

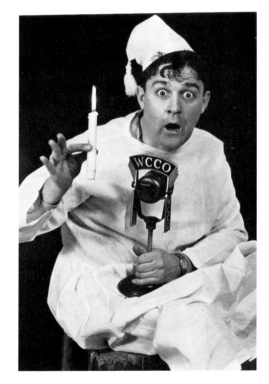

happiness as the wife of a wealthy and titled Englishman?"), *Life Can Be Beautiful* (a slum orphan girl adopted by a bookstore owner, "an inspiring message of faith drawn from life"), *Ma Perkins* (the homespun but tough widow who runs a lumberyard in Rushville Center, U.S.A.), *Portia Faces Life* (the wife of a "handsome young attorney waging a relentless war against corruption in the small city of Parkerstown"), *Joyce Jordan, M.D.*, (the "moving and dramatic story of a woman doctor—of her struggle to be a woman and a doctor at the same time.")

Listeners, to be sure, wanted more from their radios during World War II than soap suds: CBS had created its own news division in 1938 as Hitler invaded Czechoslovakia and Poland. By 1940, Edward R. Murrow was broadcasting from London almost daily during the Battle of Britain, and his CBS colleague, former Minneapolis newspaperman Eric Sevareid, was reporting from Paris during the Nazi occupation of France the same year. CBS broadcast 769 hours of news in 1940, 1,497 in 1944. "....radio alone," wrote Geoffrey Perrett, "was able to keep pace with the lurching demands of speed and direction of this helter-skelter kind of war where countries were conquered in days or hours, where the lightning bolt had supplanted the meat grinder." Given all that, it remains a puzzle that CBS would have allowed one of its owned and operated stations, WCCO, to stall until March, 1943 to establish a news bureau, and only then, apparently, under pressure from CBS' Dr. Frank Stanton. The reason may very well have been that with Adams & Co. riding high, delivering phenomenal ratings, management saw no need to spend more money on news. Wasn't it enough to have personalities read U.P. wire copy? What good would it do to pay someone to *re*-write it? When the decision was made, WCCO was fortunate to hire as its first full-time news director one of the sharpest young journalistic minds in the country, South Dakotan Sig Mickelson, who would become president of CBS News from 1954-1961. Mickelson wanted consistent control of news copy, newscasts tailored to specific interests of the WCCO listening area, time to train a staff that could deliver better copy than the radio wires. It paid off. General Manager A.E. Joscelyn discovered that news cost money to prepare, but it could make money too. "We began to see exactly what

Minneapolis Mayor Hubert Humphrey reading the Sunday comics a la Fiorello La Guardia, in August, 1946. At his left, son Skip, now Minnesota Attorney General.

45

Minnesota Governor Luther Youngdahl used WCCO Radio often in the late 1940's for his "Christian in politics" campaign against gambling and for improved mental health facilities. He also knew how to use radio with humor, calling Cedric Adams one night to congratulate him on ten years on the Night-time News with sponsor Taystee Bread:

Adams: *"Say, Governor, while I've got you now, you're a good Scandinavian. Tell me how I'm doing on my pronunciation of Svensk 'limpa' (Swedish rye bread) will you?*

Youngdahl: *You know, Cedric, with your pronunciation of 'limpa' you've prevented a lot of us from becoming psychopathic because it gives us a good laugh every time you say it. You seem to be getting a bigger kick out of it every time you say it."*

news was costing," Mickelson said years later, "....we began with a cost accounting system to price out news according to what it was costing, with a profit margin attached to it. Prior to that it had all been guesswork. But now, we put it on a businesslike basis. One of the first things I did was a complete cost-accounting analysis of what it cost us to operate and what we should charge with a profit margin attached for a minute of news at any given time of the day and with any given talent."

The bureau began, by turns, to attract attention with spot news coverage. Mickelson recalls one of its first exclusives, July 25th, 1944. An Allied carpet bombing attack in the St.-Lô area of France had killed the chief of Army Ground Forces, Lt. General Lesley J. McNair. Mickelson remembered the name. McNair was a Minneapolis native, the city even had named a street after his family. Within minutes of the wire report of McNair's death, Cedric Adams was able to lead a newscast with a report that an Army general from Minneapolis had been killed today in France. Radios began appearing on the desks of Twin Cities newspaper editors. By the end of the decade, the bureau had won the station's first Peabody award (*Arrows in the Dust*), by 1947 was producing seven five-minute newscasts a day, five 15-minute newscasts, a news analysis, a sports summary and three farm service programs.

WHAT SIG MICKELSON did for news, Larry Haeg, Sr. did for farm service. Both had Midwestern roots, both became pioneers in their professions, both rose to top management positions in the industry. Almost since its birth, WCCO had provided daily market information from South Saint Paul and the predecessor of the Minneapolis Grain Exchange, the old Minneapolis Chamber of Commerce. The station fulfilled its obligations, but just barely, so long as someone else did the work. In fact, farm leaders used WCCO to help form Land O'Lakes and Farmers Union Grain Terminal cooperatives. But now, months after Pearl Harbor, that wasn't enough. Farmers had an insatiable thirst for more sophisticated information. Under orders

Larry Haeg, Sr.

Minneapolis Tribune, April 8, 1944.

Broadcast pioneers with Midwestern roots: Sig Mickelson, Larry Haeg, Sr. and Cedric Adams at the Minnesota State Fair, 1946.

47

once again from CBS, WCCO hired a 33-year-old farmer from Plymouth in Hennepin County to be its first farm service director. Haeg had farmed his father's land during the Depression, worked for FDR's Agriculture Adjustment Administration in Washington, and helped arrange for Secretary Henry Wallace's first national network broadcast to farmers, on CBS, when Haeg realized for the first time the potential power of radio in agriculture. At WCCO, he brought before the microphone a procession of farm specialists, from county agents to plant pathologists, traveling throughout the listening area in the station's lumbering, silver and blue remote van (a converted bus). His market reports and interview programs began as public service. Within months he had his first sponsor, Jacques Seed Corn. Farm service became an important revenue producer.

For the next ten years, Haeg, who was also a member of the Minnesota Legislature, put in seven-day weeks, and in 1943 founded the National Association for Radio Farm Service Directors. With his help, WCCO Radio, for the first time, established a live, daily presence at the Minnesota State Fair, and helped strengthen 4-H and the Future Farmers of America movement.

Through the Forties, *Dayton's Musical Chimes,* the original school closing source (it began in 1934) kept its popular one hour slot at 7:30 a.m. A young copy writer with a journalism degree from Minnesota, Joyce Lamont, joined the station in 1948. It wasn't long before her elegant, feminine voice found its way on the air. CBS helped build morning audiences on WCCO with a red headed vagabond from New York City who was to become the

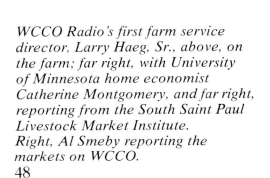

WCCO Radio's first farm service director, Larry Haeg, Sr., above, on the farm; far right, with University of Minnesota home economist Catherine Montgomery, and far right, reporting from the South Saint Paul Livestock Market Institute.
Right, Al Smeby reporting the markets on WCCO.

48

network's single most valuable property. Arthur Godfrey, like Cedric Adams, couldn't sing, couldn't dance, couldn't act, and wasn't a terribly clever ad-lib man. He was anathema to copy writers, whose work he often scorned ("Why do they give me junk like this to read?")—but listeners loved his iconoclasm and spontaneity. By the end of the decade, William Paley had completed CBS' controversial raid of talent from other networks, and Jack Benny, Red Skelton, Amos 'n' Andy and Edgar Bergen and Charlie McCarthy could all be heard on WCCO for the first time. Everything seemed secure.

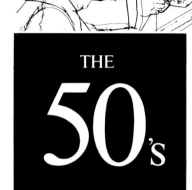

THE

50's

WABASHA, MINNESOTA

When I was a sophomore in high school in 1953 our class read Huckleberry Finn, *the story of a boy on the Mississippi River. I was a girl growing up on the same river in Wabasha, Minnesota. For the first time, it made me wonder if rivers were only supposed to be for boys. I was the only girl in a family of seven boys. Yet I felt the river was just as much mine as it was theirs. Dad saw to that. He very quietly, without fanfare, let it be known that I was to have equal opportunity. He was a doctor, one of two who ran the local clinic in the days when doctors still made house calls. We lived in one of the largest houses in town, two-story, white clapboard with green shutters, surrounded by pines, overlooking the river. Wabasha had always sort of turned its back on the rest of the world and embraced the river, nestled in bluffs like the Rhineland. The tallest things in town were the silver-gray grain elevators of the milling company, with "Big Jo" in red letters on top. The town hadn't grown or changed much in 40 years. Now it has one big supermarket, but in those days it had six small grocery stores, each delivered right to your door. The clerk in the shoe store still used a 20 foot ladder on rollers to bring down boxes from the shelves. The brown brick Anderson Hotel was a landmark even then. The cause for the greatest excitement in town in years was the changing of the toll bridge to Wisconsin to a "free" bridge. Cars lined up for miles opening day.*

Mom didn't especially care for it, but Dad saw to it that I learned to hunt and fish just like my brothers.

I remember the first time I went duck hunting. He took me and my older brother P.J. down to Weaver Swamp on the Minnesota side of the river one Sunday morning before church. I sat in a slough for about 15 minutes with him, a twelve gauge shotgun in my arms, waders up to my armpits, stocking cap almost over my eyes, freezing to death. Dad yelled to stand up. We fired at the same time at some mallards. Blam. Blam. The recoil sent me flat on my rear in the muck. A duck fluttered down. Our golden retriever "Hero" brought it back. Dad said, "It's yours, you shot it." I believed him then. I'm not so sure now.

We went trout fishing on the Whitewater, fished off the Mississippi wing dams, or Dad would take us out in his woodstrip rowboat with a seven and a half Evinrude. In the Fifties, the river was a ribbon of peace and calm, no more than half a dozen pleasure boats at any time, mostly doctors from Rochester. No wild parties on the islands. Kids didn't have boats to get there. There was even a swimming hole, Pete Bear's Gut, in a slough just down the river from our house. We grew up to the rhythm of the river and the seasons, the last barge in November, ice floes the size of buildings in late March, high water in April, the drone of dredging machines illuminated at night, lifting silt from the river bottom. My bedroom window faced the river. P.J. and I would signal at night with our flashlights and the barges would shine their blinding searchlights right back into our bedroom.

We were one of the first families in town to get a

television set. Dad and my brother Tom carried it into the living room one day, a Crosley with a 21-inch screen. It took at least a minute to warm up. We were so transfixed at first by the novelty of it that we'd get up at six just to watch the test pattern. I remember Howdy Doody, I Love Lucy, Milton Berle, Sid Caesar and Imogene Coca and the little white dot on the screen when you shut it off. But that's about all. I can't for the life of me think of a single story line.

My memory of radio in the Fifties is much more vivid. We always seemed to be doing something while we listened and the listening and doing became one. I remember Saturday afternoon in late October, 1953, raking the lawn with Dad. He had a new battery powered radio on the front steps and we listened to Michigan play Minnesota at Memorial Stadium. It was the fiftieth anniversary of the Little Brown Jug, when Paul Giel, an All American that year, ran wild, handling the ball on something like 50 plays. The Gophers won 22-0. Three people in the stands died of heart attacks in the second quarter. That's all people in Wabasha talked about for weeks because Giel was from Winona, just down the river. After the game my brothers played tackle football in the yard. Dad and I sat on the front steps. He did play by play of the game, pretending he was Halsey Hall on WCCO Radio using a rake handle as a microphone.

That was the station that was as much a part of our lives in Wabasha as the river. We woke up in the morning to First Bank notes with Jack Huston and Joyce Lamont, listened to Cedric Adams' Noon Time News when we came home from school for lunch (tomato soup). I was in bed one dark winter morning, after about a foot of snow had fallen overnight. The wind kicked up in the middle of the night. I went down to the kitchen to have breakfast. Mom was making hot cereal. I'll never forget WCCO announcing, "Wabasha, Minnesota public and private schools (pause) CLOSED." It was as if they had proclaimed the end of World War II. Radio not only tied us to the life we seldom saw in the Twin Cities, it gave us a feeling that we were part of something larger and grander than our little world.

Just before school in late summer, we'd drive to the State Fair, visit the WCCO Radio booth, watch Cedric read the news in the unbearably muggy Lee Auditorium, and look for the Wabasha County ag-extension display in the Ag-Hort building. I even remember listening to Arthur Godfrey on WCCO the morning Mom drove me down to Rochester to get my braces. More important, the older we became, was the music. In the early Fifties it was Patti Page and Doris Day, Frankie Lane and Nat Cole, Guy Mitchell and Tony Bennett. Then the rock 'n' roll explosion, Paul Anka, Frankie Avalon, Fats Domino, and Fabian. I remember hearing on WCCO the first report that Buddy Holly, Ritchie Valens and the Big Bopper had been killed in a plane crash in Iowa. Rock 'n' roll dictated not only what we listened to but what we wore, even hairstyles. Some of the guys dressed like Elvis, the girls like Annette Funicello, in cashmere sweaters, bobby socks and saddle shoes. Suddenly, everyone at school was using jazz slang: hip, cool, nice threads, "something else" and "yah know?" The movies changed us too. My favorite was "Roman Holiday" with Gregory Peck and Audrey Hepburn, which didn't make it to the Pem Theatre in Wabasha until six months after it was in the Cities. By 1957, we were reading Salinger's Catcher in The Rye. The world had changed.

The reward of radio was the way it informed you when you didn't realize it. Because WCCO was always on in our house, we absorbed the news. Alger Hiss. Joe McCarthy. "Are you now, or have you ever been, a Communist?" The Rosenbergs. Ezra Taft Benson. Korea. Sputnik. Estes Kefauver winning the Minnesota primary in 1956. I knew about all those things because the radio was always on somewhere in the house. It was an education, painless, subconscious and enlightening. Lowell Thomas at 5:45 every evening, Edward R. Murrow at 6:45, and after Halsey Hall's 10:20 p.m. sports out went the lights. Except the flashlights.

Growing up in the 1950's. The Third Grade, Douglas School, Saint Paul, 1953.

1950-1959

Sixty Years Strong

"…..*gypsy radio is ludicrously cheap. It not only dispenses with program planners, script writers, actors, sound effects men, directors and other production people, but it also reduces broadcasting to the point where only a license, a transmitter, and a subscription to* Billboard *are essential.*"

W.O. Hallaren
Atlantic Monthly
October, 1959

I N 1956, *TIME* CALLED him the "fastest rising figure in U.S. radio," a man whose "low estimate of listeners' intelligence is tempered only by his high regard for their cupidity."

In six years, 32-year-old Todd Storz had multiplied a $50,000 investment into a covey of six radio stations worth an estimated $2,500,000. In two years, he had taken KOHW in Omaha from seventh to first in the market. In Kansas City, it took him just six months to bring WHB from fourth to first. His weapon was "Top 40" radio, a format to exploit the teen-age sexual frenzy with rock 'n' roll and Elvis Presley. Teen-agers had become the fastest growing segment of Americans:

adolescents with money to spend, for the first time in their lives, on records, acne cream, clothes and cars. Storz merely gave them what they said they wanted: screaming disc jockeys, rip and read news, hit songs rotated every few hours, station jingles, and most important, cash give-aways. In New Orleans, a Storz disc jockey threw dollar bills from a rooftop during rush hour.

In Omaha and Kansas City, they conducted treasure hunts and cash calls. Wherever Storz invaded a market, he left a trail of currency. After five years of fine-tuning, he was ready to take on, head to head, one of the nation's old-line, full-service, personality stations: the venerable WCCO in Minneapolis and Saint Paul. In February, 1956, with the Edsel, payola and quiz scandals soon to be sprung on an unsuspecting public, he lit the fuse on Top 40-Cash Giveaway radio in the Twin Cities, with a line-up of widely known person-alities including Jack Thayer, Bill Bennett, Herb Oscar Anderson, Dan Dailey, and later a young movie reviewer from the *Saint Paul Dispatch and Pioneer Press,* Bill Diehl. Storz, who could almost always be seen with an earplug and a transistor, monitoring the competition, sat back to watch WDGY begin its climb from number eight in the market to number one.

For the first time in its 32 years, WCCO decided it had to fight cash with cash. It countered with

"Cash on the Line," a money give-away, and hired Minneapolis native Bob Montgomery, in his late 20s, to give the contest excitement. Montgomery's identity would be withheld from listeners, wearing a Lone Ranger mask in publicity photos. At 7:22 a.m., March 12, 1956, Big Bill Cash interrupted the news with the sound of a cash register and dialed on the air the home of Allen Brenny in the Minneapolis suburb of Richfield. A masked man giving away money on the air. In the middle of a newscast. Electric shavers paused. Buttered toast suspended in mid-chew. Car radios turned up. Brenny said, yes, he was listening and yes, he knew the key word. He won $300.00.

WCCO's Cash-on-the-line; 1956, fighting for listeners with the rock stations. Below right, Bob "Big Bill Cash" Montgomery, and below left, depositing the $125,000 prize money at the First National Bank of Saint Paul: Bank Vice President Harry E. Kern, WCCO Controller Henry E. Dornseif and General Manager Larry Haeg, Sr.

THE BATTLE HAD BEEN joined. Cash began pouring out of 'CCO Radio's heretofore penurious coffers. In one week it paid out $4,500. After six months, some $30,000. Storz raised the ante. In June, he announced that he had hidden a bank deposit note worth $105,000 somewhere in a ten-mile radius of the Twin Cities. His disc jockeys would give daily clues to its location. WCCO countered with a higher priced version of its own promotion, announcing that it had deposited $250,000 in two banks—one in Saint Paul, one in Minneapolis—to cover cash prizes to listeners that could total that amount, *if* they were listening to WCCO, of course, and *if* they knew the key word. Storz said, all right, we'll just announce the WCCO code word on WDGY, so listeners needn't tune to WCCO

to hear them. Code words changed with each WCCO call. Gleefully, WCCO switched to code phrases, such as "Tune Now to WCCO Radio" or "WCCO is Tops." WDGY swallowed hard and its disc jockeys read those phrases on the air, but soon couldn't bear to go on. There were other pitfalls for WCCO. On one occasion, two women neighbors in North Minneapolis— listening for the code word— quarreled over a $5,000 prize. One said she had given the code word to her neighbor who she claimed had agreed to split the prize after she was called. She never got her half.

A radio station that had become a friend and companion—WCCO in the 1950's: Farm Service Director Maynard Speece, Cedric Adams, Howard Viken, and Joyce Lamont.

To his credit, Storz brought WDGY to second in the market, as high as it got. By mid-April, 1956, WCCO claimed more than half a million listeners had sent in post card entries for the station's Cash Club, an extra prize game, the largest listener mail response to a single feature in the station's 32 years.

The contest, an expensive proposition, eventually stopped after raised eyebrows from the FCC, did more than help WCCO in its first serious ratings battle. "It energized all of us," said Clayt Kaufman, at the time director of promotion and publicity, "It

brought us into a new era of marketing. It told our listeners and advertisers that though we took great pride in public service and quality programming, we simply were not going to remain passive in the face of a challenge of this sort in this market. That we were going to respond in a fun and creative way." On Saturday afternoons, WCCO and Montgomery started a Top 50 countdown of hit songs, which stemmed somewhat the exodus of teen-agers to rock stations. It began *Prep Parade* in 1955, the first statewide broadcast ranking of outstanding high school teams

In the 1950's, still doing what it did best, entertaining listeners. Top, the WCCO Radio play-by-play crew for University of Minnesota football: Dick Enroth, Halsey Hall, Bernie Bierman and Sid Hartman; bottom left, "Whoopie John" Wilfarht of road show polka band fame, and bottom right, Clellan Card as Axel and his fractured "The Night Before Christmas."

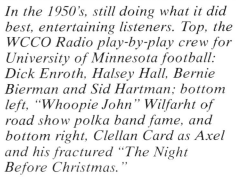

and players, a tradition that continues today.

The cash give-aways obscured a greater dilemma. By the early 1950's, radio audiences nationwide had begun to erode as television viewing increased. In 1946, an average family (there *were* average families in those days) listened to four hours and 13 minutes of radio each day. By 1953, it dwindled to two hours and 53 minutes. In 1951, CBS cut its advertising rates for network radio ten per cent for 1-8 p.m.

I T SEEMED, TO SOME affiliates like WCCO, to be a step backward. By 1952, national and local sales had replaced networks as the major source of revenue for affiliates. By 1955, CBS was forced to establish a single advertising rate for day and night. Along with most of the industry, WCCO went through an economic and psychological depression. Some skeptical advertisers deserted it for the Klieg lights of television. There was even talk in the corporate board room of moving the entire WCCO Radio operation, records, personalities and turntables, out to the transmitter near Anoka.

The change had come in 1952. TV was the catalyst. WTCN-TV was the CBS-TV affiliate in the Twin Cities. Because it owned five television stations in New York, Chicago, Philadelphia, St. Louis and Los Angeles, CBS was not permitted to own a television station in the Twin Cities. It could, however, own a minority interest in a television station. CBS therefore agreed to merge WCCO Radio with Mid-Continent Radio and Television,

Inc.'s WTCN-TV. The new company, called Midwest Radio-Television, Inc., owned WCCO Radio and the old WTCN-TV whose call letters were changed to WCCO-TV. Farm Service Director Larry Haeg was named general manager of WCCO Radio.

Midwest's principal officers, William J. McNally, scion of the Murphy newspaper family, Robert B. Ridder, the Ridder Publications, Inc. representative at Mid Continent, and F. Van Konynenburg, the operating head of WTCN, made a pivotal decision that perhaps, more than any other, contributed to the continued success of WCCO Radio. Come what may, WCCO Radio would be separate *and* competitive with its television sister; separate buildings, separate staffs, separate management. It would not occupy the caretaker's room in a television mansion.

The entire, complex transaction that merged WCCO Radio with WTCN-TV into one corporation, Midwest Radio-Television, Inc., was done without the exchange of a single penny. The former owners of old WTCN-TV, Ridder and the Minnesota Tribune Company, received a 53 percent majority interest in the new corporation with CBS getting 47 percent.

Two years later, because of FCC rule changes requiring the counting of minority interests, CBS sold its 47 percent minority interest to the *Minneapolis Star and Tribune* for $4,000,000. WCCO Radio thus became a part of the locally-owned newspapers, the *St. Paul Dispatch-Pioneer Press,* the *Minneapolis Star and Tribune* and the *Minnesota Tribune* (Murphy-McNally) interests. Television did not control the parent company.

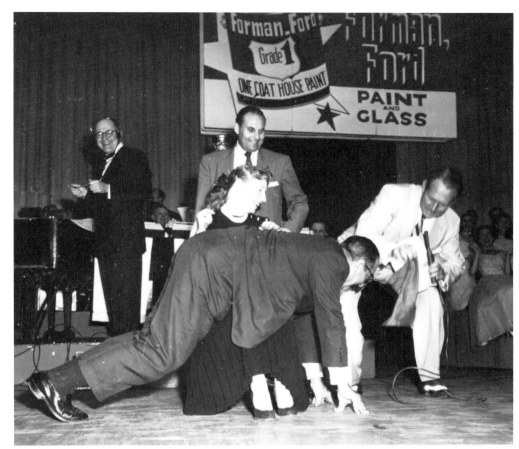

Linkletter: *Cedric, do you remember many years ago when your mother took you across her knee?*

Adams: *I, ah, vaguely recall that, yes.*

Linkletter: *Come right around here, Mrs. Franks. Your knees please. Right across. There he goes! There's the patch. There's the patch, ladies and gentlemen.*

Here's a specially sharpened needle. Now, Mrs. Franks, this is a patch about 12 inches square, and the world record is 36 seconds. This is your target for tonight.

Now ladies and gentlemen. We feel that this is an easy job. This woman could probably do this job with her eyes shut, so we'll blindfold her.

Now ladies and gentlemen, Cedric Adams has nothing to do during this stunt so I will chat with him to keep his mind off what's going on behind his back.

When I give the signal, Mrs. Franks, you start stitching. Nice, big, long, deep stitches and I'll just chat with Cedric.

Ready? Go!

Where were you born Cedric?

Adams: *Ah, in ah Adrian, Minnesota.*

Linkletter: *Do you have any brothers or sisters?*

Adams: *No, I'm an only ch....ahhhh!*

Cedric Adams and Art Linkletter at the WCCO Radio Show 1953 Minneapolis Aquatennial

Newspapers did not control it. CBS did not control it. WCCO Radio, in effect, was allowed to drift in the corporate lake and told to sink or swim on its own. The genius of keeping the WCCO stations separate, (*now* it can be called that), released a creative force at WCCO Radio in the 1950's that has become an industry legend. While some other market-leading stations stagnated under corporate control of television, WCCO was set free to find its metier—a personable, companionable radio station. It moved out of the living room and into the kitchen, the bedroom, the car, on the beach, at work, at the ball park, wherever a transistor radio (today a Walkman) could be carried. CBS Radio shifted its emphasis from entertainment and soaps, to news and information. WCCO began to assemble a line-up of some of the most talented, free-wheeling personalities in the United States, most with roots in the Midwest. To its established front line (Adams, Card, DeHaven, Hall, Ed Viehman, news analyst E. W. Ziebarth, newscaster George Grim and BBC sports refugee Stew MacPherson) it added in the 1950's: Howard Viken (1950), Allan Gray (1950), Maynard Speece (1952), Jergen Nash (1953), Jim Hill (1953), Sid Hartman (1955), Randy Merriman, Dick Chapman (1958), Charlie Boone (1959), Roger Erickson (1959) and Franklin Hobbs (1959).

Not every talent hunt was fruitful. In 1957, Program Director Bill Schwarz began casting about for a possible replacement for Cedric Adams, should he quit or retire. He contacted John Henry Faulk, the Texas humorist and broadcaster, with whom Schwarz had worked at WCBS in New York. Faulk had recently been blacklisted by AWARE, the anti-Communist organization which uses its feared bulletins to accuse broadcast performers of pro-Communist sympathy. Faulk would eventually fight the blacklist in a six year trial which won him damages of $3,500,000. Now he just wanted a job. He was invited to come to the Twin Cities all expenses paid for one week, look at housing, chat with station personalities on the air, even interview Governor Orville Freeman. He was not hired, perhaps for his gritty battle with AWARE, or because 'CCO-Land just was not ready for Texas twang and satire.

Senators Thye and Humphrey of Minnesota with Cedric Adams on WCCO Radio, early 1950's.

Clockwise: Eddie Cantor, Arthur Godfrey and Bob Hope, bringing the WCCO Radio sound to the nation on CBS in the 1950's, from the Minneapolis Aquatennial.

"Coming here we flew over Saint Paul. As you all know Minneapolis and Saint Paul are known as the Twin Cities. Twin Cities. They may have been born at the same time but Saint Paul looks as though the doctor slapped it in the wrong place. Yes sir! And when I play Saint Paul I say that about Minneapolis. Do you think that's all right?"

Bob Hope
The WCCO Radio Show at the
1953 Minneapolis Aquatennial

Abrasive and blunt though he was, Schwarz made significant changes in the sound of WCCO Radio in the late 1950's, changes that remain today. He insisted on a more human, informal sound, encouraging all air talent to emulate Cedric Adams. Once, he popped his head in the studio after a program and confronted two announcers, who shall remain nameless. "Did you think that was funny, what she just said on the air?"

"Yes," replied the announcer. "Then," said Schwarz, "why the hell didn't you laugh?"

He detested dead air. After four or five seconds of silence before the network news at the top of one hour, he dialed the studio. Jergen Nash answered. "Nash," said Schwarz, "I could have driven a truck through that dead air." Click.

It was Schwarz also who probably was the first to abbreviate the call letters to give them that distinctive, friendly informality: 'CCO.

More growth and change. In 1958, when a tornado killed 29 people in Colfax, Wisconsin, listeners responded with 50 tons of food and clothing, shipped to victims in a convoy of semi-trailer trucks. Early in the decade, WCCO Radio brought to the Minneapolis Aquatennial and the Saint Paul Winter Carnival for live broadcasts (some nationwide CBS hook-ups): Art Linkletter, Eddie Cantor, Victor Borge, Carmel Quinn, Bob Hope, Rosemary Clooney, Edgar Bergen and Charlie McCarthy and Johnny

EDGER BERGEN WCCO RADIO SHOW

Carson. In 1955, it broadcast from an Iowa farm when a bellicose Soviet premier, Nikita Khruschev, inspected hogs and corn and the best Iowa could offer on a dinner table. Its microphones were there when presidential candidates Eisenhower and Stevenson spoke at Plowville U.S.A. in Southern Minnesota.

It never stopped experimenting. In 1957, it dabbled briefly in what it called "phantom spots," short promotional phrases broadcast over programming to reach the listeners' subconscious, such as, during music, "Ike Tonight," to promote a broadcast news conference. These so-called "phantom spots" never earned money, but they could have. "We won't sell this device to advertisers," said General Manager Larry Haeg, Sr., with a qualifier, "at this time."

By the end of the decade, beyond McNally's expectations, WCCO had become the talk of radio. It

Top left, Victor Borge (second, right) with WCCO's Stew MacPherson, Larry Haeg, Sr. and Phil Lewis for a 1950's Aquatennial; left, Jack Benny, and right, Bergen and McCarthy with Cedric Adams

63

WCCO Radio News Director Jim Bormann: with Vice President Nixon, Walter Cronkite and W. Averell Harriman, a growing commitment to news and public affairs.

claimed 55.8 percent of listeners in the total service area in 1959, more than all other stations combined, and 73 percent of all listeners 6-9 a.m. Cut adrift, it had learned to swim.

Despite its commercial success in the decade, despite the competitive challenges it had met, WCCO and the rest of the industry were losing something precious in the 1950's: good radio drama and major entertainment stars. Good drama no longer paid its keep. The stars went to television. "With each program," wrote Lawrence Meyer in *The Washington Post* some 30 years later, "I gave the characters faces, dressed them up and provided them with settings and atmosphere. If I didn't like the heroine as a blonde, I could make her a redhead. No problem. But when I saw the Lone Ranger on television for the first time, I was disappointed; the actor had been picked for the wrong part... Where I pictured vast landscapes, they settled for tacky sound stages. I envisioned mansions; they provided what looked like prefabricated housing...."

Minneapolis Tribune, May 9, 1956.

With radio, no one worried about brain rot or disrupting the family… Sunday nights brought Fred Allen, Jack Benny, Phil Harris and Alice Faye, George Burns and Gracie Allen, Edgar Bergen and Charlie McCarthy, Amos 'n' Andy…And it seemed to me that when some of my friends from radio got into television, they changed somehow, became remote stars rather than the simpler folks I had known. My peers may have been impressed by all those glittering 'new' television stars, but I wasn't. I knew them back when."

Above, Larry Haeg, Sr. and Bob Dehaven sing a sponsor's tune, and WCCO Radio's smooth Gordon Eaton with singer Eddie Fisher.

65

THE
60's

FRIDLEY, MINNESOTA

Sue and I met in a chemistry class at Augsburg College in Minneapolis. We dated a few times, but lost touch during the summer. Two years later, one afternoon, after we'd both done graduate work at different schools, I gave her a call. We were married six months later at Mount Olivet Lutheran Church in South Minneapolis

We didn't waste any time starting a family. John was born in 1960. Mary, 1962. Monica at 8:30 in the morning, Friday, November 22, 1963 at Abbott Hospital in Minneapolis. I was driving from the florist to the hospital at about 12:30 listening to Jergen Nash and Maynard Speece on WCCO Radio. There was a bulletin from Dallas. Shots had been fired at President Kennedy's motorcade near Dealey Plaza. Then a bulletin that Kennedy was wounded and so was the Governor of Texas, John Connally. There was blood on the rear seat of the president's limousine. I recall a report from Dan Rather saying Mrs. Kennedy was spattered with blood. By the time I pulled into the hospital parking lot, the news came. Kennedy was dead. I woke Sue up in her room. The maternity ward, normally a happy place, was like a morgue. Radios and TV's blaring in every room. People walking with heads down.

We brought Monica home Sunday afternoon, right after the funeral and Oswald's shooting. Today I realize Kennedy's administration looks long on appearance and a little short on performance, but Sue and I felt then, and still feel, that his idealism and style and intellect were distinctive. I will remember him as he was on inauguration day, hatless in the chill, his breath visible, hand chopping the air, and those extraordinary words, "Let every nation know, whether it wishes us well or ill, that we shall pay any price, bear any burden, meet any hardship, support any friend, oppose any foe to assure the survival of liberty." We didn't know exactly then how dangerous that pledge was, but it sounded marvelous. And so, of course, did that emotional call, "Ask not what your country can do for you, ask what you can do for your country." For the first time in my life, a politician inspired me to believe that I could do great things. We decided our new baby's full name would be Monica Kennedy Carlson. After that day, the country seemed to fall apart. Vietnam. Watts. The murders of Martin Luther King and Robert Kennedy. Watergate. Would it all have happened that way if Oswald had missed? My generation is haunted by "what might have been."

The other story I have to tell took place about two years later. I do not exaggerate when I say that radio saved my life, saved Sue's life, saved the lives of John and Mary and Monica. I am more convinced of that now, almost 20 years later, than I was that terrifying evening of May 6th, 1965. We lived in Fridley, a suburb just north of Minneapolis, in a three bedroom bungalow with a two car garage, on Brookview Drive, surrounded by a lot of other heavily mortgaged three bedroom bungalows with two car garages. The weather had been humid and turbulent all week. Funnels dipping down all over the area, except the Twin Cities. We wanted to use the air conditioner at night, but didn't like the idea of not knowing what was going on outside. You wanted the radio by your bed, the reassuring calmness of Hobbs House.

I got home from work at about five that afternoon, had one of those short, chaotic dinners with Sue and the children (Monica in her high chair spilled casserole all over the floor). Then Sue and I were going to see Julie Andrews in "The Sound of Music" at the Mann Theater in downtown Minneapolis. I drove over to get the babysitter at about 5:45, and there on WCCO Radio was that familiar, unnerving klaxon horn, a tornado warning for Scott, Carver and western Hennepin counties. Just that morning, I'd been telling some people at work what a joke that horn was, how I thought 'CCO over did it. One of the columnists in the paper had called it an "electronic arsenal of blood-freezing klaxons, bleepers, high-pitched whistles, and psyched-up announcers." We snickered in agreement.

By the time I got Kathy, our babysitter, to our house the radio said not one, but several, funnel clouds had touched down in Mound and Lake Minnetonka. Possible deaths. Homes destroyed. Boats sucked right out of the water. I knew at least one thing for sure about tornadoes. They tend to move through the Twin Cities area southwest to northeast. Good Lord, were we in the path of this thing? Sue and I kept Kathy with us, pacing nervously, radios on all over the house. I walked out on the front lawn to check the horizon. The sky had an ugly dark-green hue, pressing down. The air seemed heavy. I even thought for a moment that it seemed hard to breathe. The flag on the pole in front of the Corrigans house down the block was motionless.

Ten minutes later, hail rattled on the roof, then bounced on the lawn, as big as golf balls. I looked down at my watch: 6:47. The wind rose, billowing the curtains. We opened the other windows to relieve the pressure in the house, then walked (I wanted to run) downstairs with Kathy and the children and sat in the southwest corner (I'd at least learned that much from 'CCO) and turned on our transistor radio. The next ten minutes were the most frightening of my 29 years. I discovered that all those cliches about what it feels like to be in a tornado are true. The sound of a freight train. I looked up through the cellar window and thought I saw things flying past. Far-away explosions and collisions. On the transistor, Charlie Boone or Dick Chapman or someone said, "We have a report of a touchdown in a residential area of Fridley near Highway 100 and 64th Avenue Northeast." That was us. We were right in the middle of it. The train kept roaring. I felt the house shake. Sue and I covered the kids with our bodies. Then it was over. Sue and the children were in shock and so was I. We waited a few minutes to make sure it had really passed. WCCO said there were touch downs in White Bear and Mounds View. Southwest to northeast. It made sense.

I walked up the steps, and recall that my knees were quivering. I didn't really want to open the door. If I did, would I be looking right up at the sky? The house was still there. Part of the roof was torn away over the kitchen. Windows broken. A shard of wood had impaled the living room couch. Curtains ripped. That was all.

I stood outside. The hail had almost melted into the grass. Every few minutes lightning lit up the sky and I could see the outline of the shredded remains of some of the houses on the block. The Corrigan's house was gone. Their garage was gone too; their car lying on its hood like a dead insect at the other end of the street. I smelled gas fumes. Power lines were down like snakes, moving and sparking in the darkness like Roman candles. A siren. Blinking red lights. An ambulance turned the corner. The Corrigans stayed with us that night, and the next few weeks. Next morning, WCCO Radio said the tornadoes had killed 13 people, 19 more were still missing, 400 hurt, 4,000 homeless. In Fridley alone, more than 500 homes had been destroyed. The next morning, Jim Corrigan and I walked down to what used to be his home. There was nothing left standing but a closet full of clothes. I expected him to break down but he didn't. At least we're alive, he said. Insurance will cover it. I asked would he build on the same lot or move? He looked at me and poked his foot over a gash in the lawn and he surprised me by breaking into one of his little Irish grins. "Move? Are you kidding? I just put $10 worth of fertilizer on this lawn." Men weren't supposed to hug each other in public in those days, but we embraced. It's 19 years later now. We had the Corrigans over for dinner last night. Monica Kennedy Carlson will be 21 years old this November 22nd. She asked me last night what I would think if she would apply for the Peace Corps.

Suburbia in the 60's. Cottage Grove, Minnesota, circa 1960.

1960-1969

Sixty Years Strong

"We have earned the role of personal companion. We are the link with the world for the individual listener who often feels submerged in a mass of events, a person who seeks recognition and a chance to participate in the world around him. As we pay more attention to our new role in the sixties, radio will be rewarded by a more secure place in the life of each listener."

Larry Haeg, Sr.
Speech to the National
Association of Broadcasters
San Francisco
October 21, 1960

A 63-YEAR-OLD MAN with green onion stalks in his coat pocket and a little gin on his breath plopped down in front of a broadcast microphone at Metropolitan Stadium in Bloomington, Minnesota. An awning of silky white hair fell around his bald head. His lower lip protruded slightly in a grandfatherly scowl. He had a comfortable paunch. He held a Muriel cigar, one of 18 he would smoke that day, in his right hand, which trembled slightly, depositing ash on the counter.

It was April 21, 1961, the first home game for the new Minnesota Twins, a nice day for baseball, said the fans, sunny and 63. A new American flag flapped in a gentle breeze in center field. Beyond

Halsey Hall

right field the man behind the microphone could see a new vista, the spring lemon-green of the Minnesota River Valley soon to be consumed by suburbs. Only a few years earlier, this carpet of grass between white foul lines had been a truck farm for rows of melons, sweet corn and radishes. The farmer who owned this land had lined up his machinery as a barricade on what was to become the first base line, until he received his price: $122,000 for 50 acres. Seven months before this first home game, American League President Joe Cronin had confirmed the rumors, Calvin Griffith was moving his Washington Senators to Minnesota. The announcement had come at 2:15 p.m. Twin Cities time, Wednesday, October 26, 1960 from the third floor of the Savoy Hilton in New York. "If you had told me," said Griffith, "when I got up that morning that by the end of the day we'd have a baseball team in Minnesota, I'd have told you that you were nuts." Perhaps. Days before the announcement, one story goes, Griffith was offered, besides other inducements, a sizeable commit-ment from WCCO Radio and Hamm's Beer for play-by-play rights to Twins broadcasts. Far beyond that, Twin Cities business-men had labored for almost a decade to bring major league baseball to Minnesota, paying close to a half a million dollars for the Bloomington land in May, 1955, well before talk of major league baseball became serious.

All of that made it possible for this man to come before this microphone to describe this game. There is no known recording of that first Twins game on WCCO from Met Stadium. If there were,

Baseball and radio, made for each other. Twins owner Calvin Griffith with Hall, 1961; and WCCO Radio's Howard Viken interviews Harmon Killebrew after an early Twins win.

Halsey almost certainly would be heard, in his avuncular way, "Good afternoon, ladies and gentlemen, boys and girls, from Metropolitan Stadium in Bloomington, Minnesota. This is quite a day for baseball…" It is irrelevant that the Senators beat the Twins 5-3 that day before 24,606 fans. More important is the legend of Halsey Hall that reached full flower during this decade, as the sound of his voice (and colleagues Ray Scott, Herb Carneal, Merle Harmon and Bob Wolff) carried to farm fields, back porches, factories and kitchens throughout the Northwest. In one stretch, Halsey attended more than 2,200 consecutive Twins games, home and away, describing most of them on WCCO. He had left behind his beloved newspaper work (his father had been managing editor of the old *Minneapolis Times,* and son Halsey wrote for the Star and Journal) to do Twins play-by-play.

It was a special time. Halsey at the mike, the Twins making three serious runs at the pennant in nine years. His laughter came in full-bodied waves, in rare moments perversely out of control, for baseball can often be a very funny game. It takes a person with a sense of the absurd to describe it. His mind was a bottomless reservoir of baseball anecdote. Not trivia. *Real* anecdote. Stories with a beginning, middle and end, tales and statistics with a special flavor and meaning

all their own. In a listener's mind, he became a loveable caricature. The cigars, the gin and vodka, the onions were part of the Halsey mystique. He delighted in the humor of W.C. Fields, drank to ease the fear of flying, detested spending money. Carneal remembers Halsey's questioning a bill at a Baltimore restaurant, then discovering he had left his wallet in his room. Halsey rose indignantly from the table and proclaimed to his fellow customers, "Ladies and gentlemen, *this* is a clip joint. They not only pad your check, they pick your

"I did the Starlight Salute, *10:30-11:00 p.m. and had to contend with Halsey, who did the 10:20 sports. We both worked out of studio six and Halsey always lingered so that I had to start my show talking over his shoulder while he gathered up his papers. It was a damned nuisance and I resented it. It was hard to sound properly romantic with old Halls lighting up his stinking cigars. One night, the door behind me opened. Someone was rattling around in the waste basket. It was Halsey. On the air I asked, 'Halsey—what in the name of good sense are you doing in the waste basket?' Without missing a beat, he answered, 'My boy, I am looking for my lunch.' After that night, Halsey often sat in with me. We set a new standard. Until then, broadcasting on WCCO was very precise, formal. Our badinage led to Boone and Erickson, and all the others which followed."*

Allan Gray
WCCO Radio personality.
1950's-1960's

pocket!" During a double header at Chicago's Comiskey Park, he absent-mindedly put his lit cigar in his sport coat pocket, setting fire to the jacket while Carneal gallantly continued the play-by-play in a smokey haze. 3M presented him with an asbestos sport jacket. Someone said Halsey was the only person he knew who could turn a sport coat into a blazer.

HALSEY'S HOME WAS ON

WCCO at the Met. It was a park made for baseball, cantilever design with no posts, no poles, no obstructed views. Writer Roger Angell called it an "airy cyclotron standing amid cornfields." On its turf this decade, listeners heard some of the best baseball in the nation. Harmon Killebrew would pound dozens of home runs here, watching them from home plate as an artist admiring his canvas. Rod Carew later would steal home here seven times in one season, and chase an elusive .400 batting average. The Twins would almost win a World Series over the Los Angeles Dodgers here in 1965, with wins by Grant and Kaat and a diving catch by Allison on the left field foul line. Here too would be bizarre weather: a White Sox game called because of fog in September, 1961; a Yankees game

Far left, Halsey Hall and Minnesota Twins Zoilo Versailles, Lenny Green and Harmon Killebrew, in 1962. Top left, WCCO Radio's Sid Hartman with Twins Manager Cookie Lavagetto and bottom left, the Twins win the American League pennant, 1965.

73

in early May, 1967 in 32 degrees,
17-mile-an-hour wind, wind chill
of nine above; high wind that
shook the old scoreboard and
cancelled a game with the
Senators in June that year.

That autumn of 1961, NFL
football came to Minnesota,
broadcast by Dick Enroth and Bill
Daley on WCCO Radio. Chicago's
George Halas had honored a vow
of several decades earlier to put
a team in Minnesota, and sports
entrepreneur Max Winter bought
what has become the highly
profitable Minnesota Vikings
franchise for less than a million
dollars in 1960. WCCO Radio
broadcast the first regular season
Vikings game at the Met,
September 17, 1961. NFL commissioner Pete Rozelle was in a

private box, Halas on the sidelines as coach of the Bears. A 21-year-old from Georgia, Francis Tarkenton, replaced starter George Shaw late in the first quarter, completing 17 of 23 passes for 250 yards and four touchdowns as the Vikings won 37-13. Mostly those were losing years, but Ray Christensen, who did Vikings play-by-play for WCCO Radio later that decade, remembers the *fun,* losing became an intricate adventure. Tarkenton's scrambling. Marshall's wrong way run for a safety in 1964. Five Viking laterals on the last play of one season. Joe Kapp's record-tying seven touchdown passes in one game, against the Colts in 1969. Bud Grant's first game as head coach in 1967, losing to the Cleveland Browns 42-14. Three inches of snow falling during a game with the Atlanta Falcons on December 4, 1966. The coldest game at the Met: two below zero at kick-off against the Bears on December 3, 1972, with a north wind at 11 miles an hour, a wind chill of 26 below zero. No hand warmers, no heaters allowed on the Vikings bench. The spontaneous standing ovation that greeted the Vikings back on the field at Met Stadium for the second half of the western division play-off game with the Los Angeles Rams on December 27, 1969. The Vikings rallied to win, and went on to their first of four Super Bowls. Mud. Snow. Rain. A full moon rising in the east over the final quarter of a Packers-Vikings game. Light standards swaying in the wind. "I say if your jersey ain't dirty," said Joe Kapp, "it ain't football."

Minnesota Vikings Quarterback Fran Tarkenton, Metropolitan Stadium, for a change, passing from the pocket.

The WCCO Radio on-air family in the 1960's. Bottom row: Paul Giel, Charlie Boone, Bob Allison, John Kundla, Dick Chapman, Franklin Hobbs. Second row: Ray Scott, Dr. E.W. Ziebarth, Jim Hill, Jergen Nash, Maynard Speece, Clarence Tolg. Third row: Dick Enroth, Joyce Lamont, Bob Dehaven, Roger Erickson, Paul Jay, Halsey Hall, Herb Carneal. Top row, Arv Johnson, Sid Hartman, Howard Viken, Randy Merriman, Jim Bormann and Gary Bennyhoff.

HAD HE AVOIDED politics (which seems incredible), Hubert Horatio Humphrey could have made it in radio. He did, in fact, dabble in news analysis in the 1940's opposite Cedric Adams on WTCN Radio during his formative political years. But what studio could have contained this whirlwind, this man Saul Pett said thought and talked and ran like the wind? He had been raised in an era when political speechmaking was still a decent, patriotic and free afternoon's entertainment. He had a crystal clear prairie tenor voice that cut the air. He used it from the stump like a Gatling gun (said George Will), with emotion, conviction, anger, wit and humor. He also knew how to hold a radio audience, how to coax it with cadence and rhythm, how to

deliver a thought. Tell them what you're going to tell them, said Hubert, tell them, then tell them what you told them. On television he seemed just another "talking head." On radio, where words count more than images, he was a virtuoso. From his election as mayor of Minneapolis at age 34 in 1945 to his agonizing public death from cancer at age 66 in January, 1978, WCCO Radio captured virtually every public syllable, it seemed, of his amazing career. He made a studio out of any telephone he happened to be near, in Rome, Peking, Moscow, or the American Legion hall pay phone in Granite Falls, Minnesota. And almost daily, it seemed, from the telephones just outside the U.S. Senate gallery. He knew WCCO Radio's phone number as he knew his own home's, dialed it exuberantly and often. He and WCCO Radio used one another, a mutual

admiration society that at times seemed almost incestuous. It became his personal public address system for the state. He became the station's featured attraction on hourly newscasts and Open Mike programs.

It was as if there were a spigot marked "Humphrey" in the newsroom. All an indolent newswriter had to do was turn it on. WCCO Radio often was on the road with Hubert and his entourage as he talked, thought and ran like the wind. In 1948, after a speech at Worthington's Turkey Days in southwestern Minnesota, he talked until the early morning in a hotel room with WCCO's Sig Mickelson and Larry Haeg, Sr., outlining in great detail his plan not just for election to the U.S. Senate but the Presidency. In that 1948 campaign, a then-Democrat named Ronald Reagan endorsed him in a broadcast on WCCO Radio. In 1958, WCCO Radio News Director Jim Bormann accompanied him to the Soviet Union, and a surprise five-hour meeting with Premier Khruschev at the Kremlin. He returned home to find his portrait on the cover of *Time,* his name mentioned as a serious contender for the 1960 Democratic nomination for President. In April, 1960, Bormann and Dick Chapman covered Humphrey's battle with John F. Kennedy in the Wisconsin presidential primary.

Hubert Humphrey, never "mike-shy." Late 1940's, with WCCO Radio News Director Sig Mickelson and Dr. E.W. Ziebarth and the 1960's at a Twins game with Merle Harmon, Herb Carneal and Halsey Hall.

SO IT CAME TO BE that Hubert was on WCCO at the turning point of his career. It was August 26, 1964. He happened to be taking part in a WCCO Radio listener call-in show from Atlantic City during the Democratic National Convention. It was 1:30 p.m. Twin Cities time. For months, President Johnson had been orchestrating the charade of choosing a running mate. Humphrey's liberal Minnesota colleague in the Senate, Eugene McCarthy, had just removed his name from contention. Humphrey

was the only logical choice. He chatted with listeners from his ninth floor suite at the Shelburne Hotel, overlooking Boardwalk and Ocean, vases of red and white carnations throughout the room, Bormann nearby with a tape recorder. Reporters jammed the corridor outside. How is Muriel?, asked one caller. How is Atlantic City? asked another. Homey stuff. *Meet the Press* it was not. Then, a CBS Netalert bulletin with the voice of Dan Rather seized the air. President Johnson, strolling with reporters on the White House grounds, said he was going to call Humphrey and invite him to Washington.

"Senator," said Roger Erickson on the air after the bulletin, "I really didn't know anything about this."

"Neither did I," said Humphrey, "but it indicates to me that I'd better get off the phone…I don't want the President to call and find the line is busy…a fellow could miss the train."

Four years later, Humphrey's voice cracked on WCCO from the Leamington Hotel in Minneapolis as he conceded the presidential election to Richard Nixon by a margin of one-tenth of one per cent of the votes cast. In

Vice President Humphrey, far left, in Atlantic City, with WCCO Radio, and, left, speaking to the Minnesota Grain Terminal Association, Saint Paul, 1966.

January, 1969, he made world news in an interview on WCCO, saying he had become tired of his advisers in the campaign and had kicked them all out of a hotel room to decide for himself to break with Johnson over the bombing of North Vietnam. Nine years later he was dead, after being elected to the Senate twice, after the first public disclosure of his inoperable cancer, after his final journey to Washington and his farewell to Congress, emaciated by cancer, cheeks sunken, hair thin and white from chemotherapy. All of it chronicled in sound on WCCO, right down to the funeral, which he himself had planned and seemed present at....somewhere.

"Let there be no eulogy," he had said a few days before his funeral, "I have had enough eulogy for two

WCCO Radio General Manager Larry Haeg (center) presents the 1966 Minneapolis Chamber of Commerce Farm Forum report to

U.S. Agriculture Secretary Orville Freeman and President Lyndon Johnson at the White House.

lives. Instead, let us have a celebration of life for me, for my family, and for the people of the little towns all over Minnesota. And let us have congregational singing, and music, and happiness! No sympathy for me. I've had a wonderful life."

IN 1960, WARNER Brothers released an album by a comic named Bob Newhart, a Jesuit-educated Chicago man, and erstwhile certified public accountant. One of the routines on the album was called the "Driving Instructor," the five-minute saga of Mrs. Webb and the man who tried to prevent her self-destruction behind the wheel. Something strange happened. The album virtually disappeared from major markets across the nation. Warner Brothers found itself shipping almost every available copy to record stores in Minneapolis-Saint Paul. It was there that the most popular radio personality in the Northwest, Howard Viken of WCCO Radio, had taken a liking to it, playing it every morning to an unprecedented response from listeners. In only two weeks, in the Twin Cities' metro area alone, Viken recalled, listeners to WCCO had purchased 3,000 copies a day of "The Button Down Mind of Bob Newhart." The response triggered a nationwide demand for the album and helped launch Newhart's career. "All right. There we are," said the driving instructor, "Let's get up a bit of speed. That's the way. Now let's practice some turns. Ah, the important thing on turns is not to make them too sharp. Just kind of make a gradual.....oh, now that was fine. That, that was a wonderful turn....it, it's hard for me to believe you've only had two lessons after you make a turn like .....are you sure you haven't had more now? I find that very difficult to believe. One little thing. Ah, this is a one way street. Well, now, no....actually it was partially my fault you see. You were in the left hand lane and you were signalling left and ah, I just more or less *assumed* you were going to turn left. Ah, same....same to you fella!"

Howard Viken had come to WCCO Radio ten years earlier and almost left soon after when another station in the Twin Cities offered him more money and his own show. Almost 30 years later, Viken recalled that Bob DeHaven told him not to take the offer. "He reminded me," said Viken, "this was one of the top three stations in the country. He told me to be patient and good things would happen to me. He said, 'Howard, if you'll just be patient and get a regular time slot in the morning, all you'll have to do is hiccup on the air and you'll become famous." In 1984, Howard Viken began his 35th year of broadcasting with WCCO Radio.

R ADIO PROVED resilient. FCC Commissioner Newton Minow, in 1960, the year Viken played Newhart, called radio "America's roommate… America's traveling companion. It travels with us like a welcome shadow." By then, almost 100 per cent of adults in America lived in homes with radios. Forty-five percent of adults still listened to

Howard Viken (far left) with Irish singer Carmel Quinn in the 1960's, and below, reunited with Bob Newhart, 1982.

The master of "one to one" radio, Arthur Godfrey, visits WCCO Radio for its 40th anniversary in 1964, with Howard Viken, Charlie Boone, producer Bill Balch and Roger Erickson. Opposite page, Erickson covers the 1965 Fridley tornado damage.

radio daily. WCCO reached unprecedented peaks in market dominance. In the autumn of 1962 it claimed a 68.1 percent share of the Twin Cities area listeners, twice as many listeners as all other Twin Cities' stations combined. Four years later it claimed its morning audience was larger than the prime time evening audience of any television station in the Twin Cities. In 1965, it won Peabody, Dupont and Sigma Delta Chi national awards for public service and natural disaster reporting of tornadoes, floods and blizzards. "On the Go with 'CCO" became the slogan of the

60's: broadcasting, for instance, from the North Pole in April, 1968 when Ralph Plaisted's Minnesota expedition made the first journey on the Earth's surface to 90°N.

The old made way for the new. It was not always a joyous transition. Cedric Adams died at age 59 in February, 1961. Four years before his death he had said, "I'm strictly a provincial and enjoy every minute of it and want to remain that way." The year before, the last of the CBS Radio network soaps, *Ma Perkins,* went off the air on WCCO on November 25th, after 7,065 broadcasts. Virginia

Payne had played Ma on every show, beginning at age 23, ending at age 50. "If you'll write to me, Ma Perkins, at Orleans, Massachusetts," she said on the final broadcast, "I'll try to answer you. Good-bye, and may God bless you." *Gunsmoke* followed in 1961, *Yours Truly, Johnny Dollar* in 1962, the last major dramatic show on network radio and WCCO.

Through the decade, some changes were obvious, some almost imperceptible. The station's news, information, weather and sports commitment broadened, so did the range of music it played, from soft rock to light classics. A farm boy from Winthrop, Minnesota and a well-traveled cosmopolite from Connecticut, California and Colorado, came together by chance in the afternoons to form what would become one of American radio's most durable personality teams: Boone and Erickson. Sportscaster Ray Christensen and former college football All American and major league baseball pitcher Paul Giel arrived in 1963, the year the first WCCO Radio Good Neighbor award went to former NATO chief and Minnesota native, Lauris Norstad. A farm auctioneer and father of seven from Duluth, Chuck Lilligren, arrived in early 1965 and a few months later, among other duties, did a show from 12:15 to 5:00 a.m. Monday, making WCCO for the first time a seven day a week, 24 hour a day broadcasting service. From Duluth also came the textured, friendly voice of Joe McFarlin,

the man of many dialects and yarns. Three years later, the entertainment editor of the *Saint Paul Pioneer Press and Dispatch,* with 20 years experience in print and broadcasting, joined the staff. Bill Diehl was fond of telling the story of the woman who approached him at the station's broadcast center at the Minnesota State Fair ten years later. The woman asked his name, and when told, replied, "Oh, you're the *new* one." Acceptance takes time.

"Funny things result from some broadcasts. My wife went to a club meeting the other day and a friend of hers said, 'You know, it's funny the things men won't do.' My wife said, 'Well, what did your husband do now?' 'Well,' she said, 'the other day he came home dragging a five pound bag of whole wheat flour to make gravy with. He heard some fellow telling about it on the radio.' I was the fellow—my wife never told her."

Uncle Fogy (Clarence Tolg)
WCCO Radio personality
in the 1960s and early 1970s
from "The Lore of Uncle Fogy"

THE 70's

RICE LAKE, WISCONSIN

My decision to leave the Twin Cities came not in the middle of a traffic jam on Highway 12 during rush hour, but over several years, perhaps back to my last year of law school at Minnesota. It was not an easy decision. I had invested seven years in a respected, medium-sized Minneapolis law firm, swimming upstream in the old boys' network. Minneapolis-Saint Paul magazine even did a half page "People to Watch" feature on me as a "savvy lawyer commanding respect in major litigation, known as well for her active community involvement." Dad sent copies to all the relatives. I was on the way up. Near the end I was pulling a six figure salary, investing half of it after taxes, having business lunches with the pinstripe crowd at the Blue Horse and Charlie's (when there was a Charlie's). I had also become serious with Don, a vice president at Honeywell. I was born and raised in South Minneapolis in a modest two-story stucco home three blocks from the east shore of Lake Harriet, went to Southwest High and Minnesota. Minneapolis was in my blood. I am not a radical feminist, nor am I terribly active in politics. I prefer to carry on quietly but firmly.

I did not leave the Twin Cities for the usual negative reasons which emigres give. Actually, I often found the pace of life in the Cities stimulating. Looking back, I left for reasons partly selfish. It came one night when I read the late Sigurd Olson's Reflections from the North Country. *"When one finally arrives at the point where schedules are forgotten," he wrote, "and becomes immersed in*

ancient rhythms, one begins to live." At age 35, it was that part of life I wanted to find, not an end in itself but a way to touch those around me in a deeper way. I did not see myself running from responsibility, as Don claimed, but toward it. That was one of the troubles with life in the Cities, my inability to know even a handful of people in an honest way. I do best one to one with people, not contrived babble at cocktail parties. One can feel terribly alone in the singles crowd at the Loon Cafe, and occasionally desperate. Everyone is acting, posing.

For a couple of years I had scoured certain areas of the north in a desultory way, telling no one, not even my parents or Don. I found a small, friendly town in northwestern Wisconsin called Rice Lake (population 7,300) about a three hour drive from the Cities. My parents once had a summer cabin in that area so I knew the territory. Far enough to be away, close enough for a taste of what I feared I might miss. There was room for a small legal practice there, enough to pay the bills. I found a cabin on a nearby lake.

I left the Cities July 30, 1975. The radio in my green Volkswagen beetle played the Carpenters ("Close to You") and told of the disappearance of Jimmy Hoffa in Michigan. I had a melancholy dinner with Don the night before at Saint Anthony Main looking at the twinkling Minneapolis skyline across the river, and a good-bye the next morning with Mom and Dad.

Sign posts. Forest Lake. A semi's wake shook the car. Chisago City. A young mother (brief envy) *pushing her baby in a stroller down a sidewalk in Lindstrom. Center City. This was a new home for Scandinavian immigrants a century ago. A young blonde boy driving a tractor on the side of the road, probably one of their descendents. Taylors Falls, the worn auburn cliffs above the Mississippi, and into Wisconsin. I made certain I had a full tank of gas before leaving the Cities. The Arab oil embargo hit the previous fall, regular was up to $1.30. There were lines at stations lucky to have supply left near the end of the month. Another good reason, I thought to myself smugly, to be out of the rat race.*

The first few weeks were lonely, as I knew they would be. Gradually, the town accepted me, and I became a regular along with the rest of the locals at the main street coffee shop early on weekday mornings, a few merchants, dairy farmers, retirees and the editor of the paper. Ida, the waitress, called me by my first name after the second week, a small triumph. I joined the choir at the Lutheran church.

It was a crisp, radiant autumn; maples, oaks and birch put on a glorious display. The scent of pine and woodsmoke. When I wasn't working late at the office, I was out at the cabin, learning how to tame the woodstove, caulking cracks in the cabin walls, doing some amateur plumbing. There were morning walks alone on a horse path near the fogged lake, with a cup of fresh coffee in the chill morning air. A few deer. Chickadees. Red wing blackbirds. No television. Sometimes a newspaper. I had packed a radio, the beat-up leather one I'd had since college with AM and short wave. Mom put it in one of my suitcases as an afterthought. One day at the hardware store I bought batteries for it, placed it on the sill above the kitchen sink, the window with a view to

the lake. I put it there mostly as nostalgic bric-a-brac, the old fashioned dial brought back memories of cramming for tests through the night in college. One morning around 9:30 I was doing dishes and wondered if it still worked. I reached up with a sudsy hand, clicked it on and went up and down the AM dial through the static for something to listen to. One station came in clear, the friendly and vaguely familiar voice of a man I couldn't place. He played a Dionne Warwick song and then said that he agreed with something called Quigley's Law: "If you take off your left hand glove in the winter, your car keys will be in your right hand pocket." I laughed. I hadn't laughed in that little girl way in months, and here a man who I couldn't remember, and couldn't see, had made me do it. Howard Viken? Was he still around? I hadn't heard his voice for it seemed twenty years. Then he played David Rose's "The Stripper" to introduce Joyce Lamont (I hadn't heard her in twenty years either). I laughed again at something he said. What am I doing, I thought, laughing at this man playing this sexist music and telling these stupid jokes? Then she spent three minutes giving a recipe for oatmeal pie: two eggs, beaten, one cup sugar, 1/2 cup light corn sugar, 3/4 cup quick-cooking oats... The voices, the music, the laughter, the old fashioned recipe for oatmeal pie, it seemed to fit my mood like an old shoe. It belonged with what I was doing. It didn't intrude, offend, jar or aggravate. It seemed like an old friend found. I wrote Howard a letter as soon as I'd finished the dishes and told him to knock off the stripper music. He should know better.

Minnehaha Falls, Minneapolis.

1970-1979
Sixty Years Strong

"It's like a great hotel. You can't build a great hotel, you have to develop it. You don't invent the Dorchester Hotel. WCCO Radio is a way of life. If a bomb went off here, I think our audience would switch to WCCO to find out about it. To try to overtake them would be trying to break down 50 years of a part of the culture of this area."

Gary Stevens
Twin Cities radio executive
March 30, 1976

"WCCO Radio…is a comfortable sort of place where everything in sight is anywhere from 5 to 50 years out of date. It is a confirmation of expectations. There are the corny plaques and awards on the walls, the rooms stacked floor to ceiling with fraying record jackets, the harried but coolly-efficient engineers, the hustling, earnest young newsmen dashing purposefully from room to room grasping slips of paper, the receptionist who looks like everybody's sister…and of course, the announcers, the names we grew up with…At WCCO Radio it's as though the Fifties and Sixties never happened, and on reflection perhaps that's not so bad. In a day of fakey plastic nostalgia this is the real thing."

David A. Peterson
Minneapolis magazine
June, 1974

"You must be the nice folks who wanted to tour our studio."

Cartoonist Richard Guindon's gentle view of the "Good Neighbor's" lobby, 1975. (Reproduced by permission of the Minneapolis Star and Tribune.)

SOME RADIO OLD-TIMERS thought it a sacrilege. It was as if someone had thrown a rock through a stained glass window, littering the ground with fragments of a masterpiece. Yet it was inevitable and necessary. The 1970's found radio in a fragment of formats, each an exaggeration, in some ways, of the whole: adult contemporary, news-talk, country, religious, hard rock, soft rock, big band, "music of your life" nostalgia, jazz, album-oriented rock, variety-personality, classical, beautiful music, Black, Hispanic, "listener supported" public radio. Together they offered listeners diversity and choice, but also threatened the market dominance of the traditional, mass appeal stations such

as WCCO. They were a la carte. WCCO was a smorgasbord. They were narrow-casting. WCCO was, literally, *broad*casting. Would there still be a need for a radio station that tried to be almost all things to almost all people, trying to offer something for almost everyone, September wheat futures one moment, Paul McCartney and Wings the next, two commercials, and a Norwegian fiddler on Syttende Mai the next?

Fragmentation already had destroyed mass appeal magazines such as *Colliers, Life* and *Look*. When the venerable *Saturday Evening Post* went under after 147 years and losses of $18,000,000 in one year, its publisher confessed

Boone and Erickson, circa 1974, masters of dialect: "We do everything except American."

out loud in early 1969, "Apparently there is just not the need for our product in today's scheme of living."

Well, just what *was* the "scheme of living" that changed radio and WCCO in the 1970's? It was, first, a result of World War II: more women entering the work force. More career women trying to be mothers. More women living alone. More divorces. Fewer marriages.Child custody battles, as portrayed in Avery Corman's *Kramer vs. Kramer,* became almost a way of life.

Radio was changing because its listeners were changing. More day care centers, fast food restaurants, microwaves, and "soup for one." More single parent households. Listeners became sophisticated consumers. Country western and rock segmented music tastes. The service economy expanded at the expense of manufacturing, shrinking the middle class. The economic ground began to shift under society's most stable unit: the family. The Arab oil embargo

"Just Folks Radio." Minnesota Governor Al Quie udderly amazed at Roger Erickson at the WCCO Radio broadcast center at the Minnesota State Fair; and above, the warm, friendly presence of Howard Viken.

made gasoline and petroleum precious liquid. There were fewer farms (Minnesota alone lost 71,000, down to 118,000, between 1945 and 1974). More elderly lived alone, isolated from their children. Church attendance declined. More Americans depended on the redistribution of the nation's wealth through social service programs: Medicare, AFDC, food stamps and Social Security. The billions poured into the desperation of Vietnam had sapped the strength of the American economy.

FRAGMENTED RADIO formats were also the result of the astounding growth of FM stations, stunted for decades by economic forces beyond their control. FM's multiplied, became commonplace in car receivers and stereo head-sets, began to dominate almost every major market in the nation. In 1964, FM's had annual revenues of only about $20,000,000; by 1974, some $224,000,000. Major commercial network dominance in radio and television eroded too,

Far left top, Jergen Nash, the voice of WCCO Radio News in the 1970's; and above, another respected veteran, WCCO Radio government correspondent Arv Johnson.

Veteran Engineer Art Johnson, part of WCCO Radio's outstanding technical staff behind the scenes, at master control. "I've known reporters to get excited but never an engineer," wrote Edward R. Murrow. "When things go wrong and a broadcast fails to get through, they just shrug their shoulders and say, 'It's leaving here all right.' Engineers are the toughest critics in radio and for this reporter it's a very great day when an engineer says, 'That was a pretty fair piece.'"

victims of pay cable, direct broadcast satellite, UHF, video cassette recorders, low power television, and special interest networks. Proliferating sources of entertainment on television and radio allowed listeners and viewers to be their own program directors. Many American homes became what futurist Alvin Toffler called the "electronic cottage."

Quantity did not guarantee quality. In some cases, a Gresham's law of broadcasting was at work: imitators sprung up, copying successful formats, some committed only to greater profit not public service, diminishing the influence of stations which had a clear sense of their public mission. A trip up and down the AM and FM dials began to sound like an echo chamber. One word described it: clutter. Stations struggled to maintain their identity in the marketplace, to "position" (as the catch-phrase went) themselves among their competitors. Image had become more than content. "Too often the machine runs away with itself," William Paley had said in 1936, "instead of keeping pace with the social needs it was created to serve."

Present and future Hall of Fame members. Left, Boone and Erickson with Harmon Killebrew, live from Twins' spring training at Orlando, Florida, and above WCCO Radio's Sid Hartman with Rod Carew at Met Stadium.

WCCO Radio remained dominant enough early in the decade to attract nation-wide attention. A textbook on modern American radio programming devoted an entire sub-chapter to the station. "From the tables down at Murray's on Sixth Street to the most remote northwoods hamlet," said an article in the *National Observer*, "people are listening to WCCO and loving it." A column-left article in the *Wall Street Journal* in April, 1973 ("Just Folks Radio") said the station dominated its listening area like no other station in the country. If the winds of change are blowing at 'CCO, it said, they're not blowing very hard. Indeed, the station made few changes in the 1970's. The changes it did make proved wise. In 1969, it hired a 23-year-old out of Winona, Steve Edstrom, who became the brightest young radio

voice in the region. On board too came a young Dan Hertsgaard of Minneapolis, the station's first second-generation air personality.

It also made, in 1971, the most radical departure in choice of air talent in the station's history. It hired the highly talented vagabond, Steve Cannon, native of the Minnesota Iron Range, keeper of one of the most beguiling character menageries in American radio: Ma Linger (she of high heels and singles bars), Morgan Mundane (sports editor of the Congressional Record, resident of the seedy Fairmont Hotel) and Backlash LaRue (an effeminate advertising account executive who patronizes an exclusive outdoor apparel shop in Glendive, Montana). What he lacked in

Roger Erickson and friend, the Vice President's mansion, a live broadcast, January, 1979.

warmth and sensitivity, he more
than made up for in wit and
presence. His burly, side-of-the-
mouth voice filled up the radio
stage, appealing to a younger
demographic. Like Boone and
Erickson, his style was neo-golden
age radio, a revival of the sound
and word imagery of the 30's and
40's, in the tradition of Allen's
Alley or the one-to-one approach
of master salesman, Arthur
Godfrey. Cannon could be
irreverent, iconoclastic, gruff,
but above all, he communicated,
whether a listener liked him or
not. With a 50,000-watt clear
channel signal and 'CCO's market
acceptance behind him, gradually
he came to command one of the
largest shares of afternoon drive
time audience in a major market
in the nation. Boone and Erickson
did the same in the morning. It
was radio the way Dave Garroway
had wanted it on NBC's *Monitor:*
"I promise you that in this hour
there will be at least one moment
of fascination."

I T BECAME A TURBULENT
decade for WCCO Radio News,
the listeners' ear for 45 hours of
live coverage via CBS Radio of

six days of the Senate Watergate committee hearings in 1974, the return of prisoners of war from Vietnam, the occupation of Wounded Knee, South Dakota by militant Indians, the Rapid City flood, a Nobel peace prize for Minnesota agronomist Norman Borlaug, and four frustrating Super Bowls for Bud Grant's Minnesota Vikings. It was a decade for leave-taking too, the deaths of Hubert Humphrey and Halsey Hall, the end of Lowell Thomas' 46 years of newscasting in 1976, when, at age 84, he uttered for the last time on a night in May on WCCO Radio, "So long."

On October 2, 1974, WCCO Radio celebrated its 50th anniversary, duly noted later in a novel, *The Cavanaugh Quest,* by Minnesota's Thomas Gifford: "It was a pearl-gray morning with mist hanging like a netting from the trees of Loring Park [said protagonist Paul Cavanaugh, an investigative reporter]. I had an early appointment with Bernstein at the courthouse, where he worked in a tight little office just off the squad room, a floor beneath the slammer itself. The traffic was sorting itself out more slowly than usual and I listened to WCCO, the ubiquitous radio station, which was indulging itself in an orgy of self-congratulation on its fiftieth birthday. They were working on my kind of music, the kind you don't hear anymore. Somebody with a mean sax was playing 'At Last' and I remembered the words from a long time ago." At age 50, it was still radio as it was supposed to be, "the kind you didn't hear anymore."

The Minnesota Vikings in the 1970's, one of the NFL's most successful franchises: far left, Fran Tarkenton and Bud Grant; left, Dave Osborne and above, Jim Marshall.

THE

80's

THE TWIN CITIES

The red, digital numbers on the radio alarm glowed on my pillow: 5:07 a.m. A crack of light from the bathroom. The rustle of her running suit. Rain tapped the roof. I managed a groggy mumble.

"Sarah, please, don't go out in that stuff."

"Got to."

"Why?"

"You know why. I've got to get my miles in."

"Why don't you do it this afternoon?"

"Can't. Too busy."

"You're stupid," I said, and turned over in bed.

She clicked off the light and bent down to kiss me. "I'm doing 12 miles. Change Andrea's diaper and get her dressed. Daniel will be up in about an hour and needs a feeding. There are waffles for you in the freezer." She tiptoed down the stairs, the front door opened and closed. I drifted off. The alarm went off at 6:07, in the middle of the Good Morning song on WCCO Radio. Roger Erickson was telling another Norwegian joke in dialect. "…so the store owner says, 'Well, why do you want exactly 12 pairs of underwear?' and the Norwegian says, 'Vell, dere's Yanuary, February, March…'" I bottle fed Danny in the living room, with the CBS Radio World News Round-Up. Reagan campaigning. Interest rates up. Personal spending down. Was our Dayton's bill paid? Sarah dripped in, her dark hair in wet ropes, pink running suit soaked.

"How'd it go?"

Danny burped.

"Fine. Wasn't raining that hard." She was on her back, bringing her legs straight up together and back, toes touching the carpet behind her head. Her face reddened, blood vessels appeared on her temples, as she stretched. She grunted, "Is Andrea up?"

"She's watching cartoons."

"I thought we said no TV on weekday mornings."

"I know, but once won't hurt. It's nice to have quiet while I feed Danny."

"Welcome to the club."

"Did we pay our Dayton's bill?"

"I sent it yesterday. Let's not charge for a while, we owe them $325."

Howard Viken was reading the news, time to shower and shave. I didn't tell her often enough, how I admired her discipline. To think I was the one who got her into running. Now it was early September, and she was putting in her last few weeks of training before the Twin Cities Marathon on the 30th. She'd been running for three years, done a lot of 10K's (her best wasn't bad, 46:30) and a half marathon, now she wanted to see if she had 26.2 miles in her. Dick Chapman was reading the morning Almanac (the 12th anniversary of the Munich massacre) and the Good Neighbor award (a woman retiring after 30 years as a teacher in Canby, Minnesota). I found Andrea in the kitchen eating cereal, dwarfed by the yellow, family size Cheerios box.

"Andrea, only pour what you can eat. Can you eat all that?"

"Sure. Where's Mommy?"

"Taking a shower."

"Why didn't you run, Daddy?"

"I know better."

Boone and Erickson were on, calling someone in London, then a skit on a home for unwanted zucchini, "nature's own Xerox machine." A discussion followed about printing World Series tickets. A story from California about a beer just for homosexuals called "Oscar Wilde." Would you, Roger wondered, pour it into a Gertrude Stein? It was virtually the only station we listened to since coming here. Sarah and I were raised in California, came here four years ago when 3M transferred me with our two adopted Korean children, Andrea, 5, Danny, seven months. We bought a home near Portland and Minnehaha Parkway in South Minneapolis not far from the creek. We now have a Minnesotan's arsenal in the garage to fight winter: shovels, no snow blower yet, ice scrapers, anti-freeze, jumper cables, winter weight oil, cross country skis. Andrea spilled orange juice on Sid Hartman's column in the Star and Tribune. I mopped it up. I yelled upstairs. "Sarah, I'm late. See you tonite."

"Okay. I'm taking the kids to their check-up today. Won't be home til maybe five."

In the car, Boone and Erickson were talking with naturalist Jim Gilbert about signs of autumn. Northern Orioles had begun to migrate. It looked now, he said, as if the peak of fall colors would be around the end of the month. Just in time, I thought, for the marathon.

* * *

It was an ungodly hour to get up with the kids. We drove through the darkness. 35W almost deserted. Andrea and Danny slept in the back seat. Joe McFarlin on WCCO said it was 45 above with a slight breeze from the northwest. The stars were out. A clear sky. A hint of sunrise. Linda Ronstadt sang "What's New?" Streetlights were still on in downtown Minneapolis. We turned the corner on Marquette to head up 6th and found…what can I say? A circus? A block party? The streets alive with

thousands of people, bands playing, runners nervous in warm-up suits. The Pillsbury Center jammed with stretching figures, their families and friends mingling in knots of ministry to the runners. Some had just come from a worship service at Saint Olaf's Catholic Church, for runners of all faiths. I thought of Saint Paul, "….I have finished the race," in the Bible. Sarah safety-pinned her number (5068) to her turquoise running top. I tried lamely to ease her jitters.

"Thirty-two year old mother of two wins Twin Cities Marathon. Details at 10," I said, a not-too-good imitation of Ted Baxter.

She barely smiled, "and loses her cookies at mile 20."

Have you had enough water? She nodded. Vaseline? Yes.

It was the first marathon I'd ever seen. Race director Jack Moran barked orders on the p.a., his voice echoing off the government center. The blank pistol fired into the air at 7:15 sharp. The start was unforgettable: enormous, street-wide trunks of humanity undulating slowly up Second and Third Avenues. A sea of bobbing heads. Smiling faces, grim faces, ecstatic faces, uncertain faces. Runners waving. Sixteen thousand feet floating over the pavement. Wheelchair athletes started earlier. I thought I saw Sarah at one point but wasn't sure. We got in the car and headed for the west shore of Lake Calhoun. We should see her there around 8 a.m., if she did nine and a half minute miles. Someone was playing the theme from the movie, "Terms of Endearment" on a loudspeaker near mile three—running music. The red and white WCCO Radio van came into view ahead of the lead runners; smooth, fluid, fully-extended strides, like gazelles. We had our radio on. The sun had risen on the lake, reflecting off the leaves in a blur of color, silhouetting geese and mallards. The crowd grew along the curb, three deep in spots.

Andrea yelled, "There's mommy! Mommy!" She glided past, looking effortless, a huge smile. Forgetting the kids, I ran alongside on the grass. "You're too fast! Don't push too hard! Save something!" We jumped in the car, folded Danny's stroller, to mile ten on the Parkway, the scene repeated. She looked good. Mile 15 just before Summit Avenue in Saint Paul. Her face flushed a little now. Arms moving a little above her waist. Radios everywhere, almost a canyon of sound. The WCCO Radio van and the lead runners already had crossed the finish line near the state capitol, but the real race was here. Almost three hours now since the start. We watched her round the corner to come up onto Summit again after the last hill on Lexington Parkway. 3:33:15. She favored her right leg, and the sore knee that had bothered her. "If you have to walk, then walk,

that's okay!" I yelled.

"Maybe!" She was in her own private agony now. On her own, which is the way she wanted it.

The lime green digital numbers clicked above the finish line banner in front of the state capitol. People leaning out of windows, 10 deep on the boulevard. Somehow we squeezed up front. It was like a ticker tape parade. Andrea tried to tell me something but I couldn't hear above the roar. Danny started to cry, frightened by the noise. A block away, in a clutch of runners, straining every muscle, was a blush of turquoise. I remember thinking there is a lot more to life than this crazy race, but for the moment it was quite enough.

Pinchas Zucherman directs the Saint Paul Chamber Orchestra, 1983

1980-1984
Sixty Years Strong

"*I would call (WCCO Radio) The World's Greatest Backfence Chat. Who else would you phone to report seeing 45 eagles just north of Winona? Or phone to say your kid was perfect in spelling? The interesting thing is that it would be simply impossible to invent WCCO. Everyone would think you were crazy.*"

William Sumner
Associate Editor
Saint Paul Dispatch
and Pioneer Press, 1983

IMAGINE YOUR KITCHEN radio is an electronic Aladdin's lamp, creating in your midst, like Star Wars holograms, the characters of the voices one hears throughout the day on WCCO Radio.

What a bizarre procession it would be.

An eccentric Norwegian janitor with a cackle laugh, baggy pants and gold-rimmed spectacles (Roger Erickson's "August"); a Southern politician with white mustache, cream-colored tails and white hat (Charlie Boone's "The Senator," patterned after the Kenny Delmar character of Allen's Alley); a newspaper advice columnist with polyurethane

After 25 years together, the highest rated morning radio team in a major market in the United States. Boone and Erickson and their intersection sign in the Minneapolis suburb of Brooklyn Park, 1981. (Reproduced by permission of the Minneapolis Star and Tribune.*)*

hairdo and high-pitched lisp (Tim Russell's "Ann Panders"); a grouch in a vest and snap-brimmed fedora with a bookie's tip sheet firmly in fist (Steve Cannon's "Morgan Mundane.")

Is this 1924, or 1984 or some year between?

It is, really, all those years. This story began in 1924 with a person, a microphone, an invisible audience and the human imagination. We have, in one sense, come no further. Good radio remains time-*less*, a simple equation for complex times. Sixty years have come and gone, or have they? "Sometimes a man's experience is like the sweep second hand on a clock," wrote William Least Heat Moon in *Blue Highways,* "touching each point on its circuit but always the arcs of a movement repeating."

Perhaps this is what confuses network executives from the coasts, consultants from media capitals, when they visit the Twin Cities and listen to WCCO Radio in their hotel suites. They are baffled: *this* is the great WCCO Radio?

Eager to covet the future, they neglect the past. The past of WCCO Radio is contained in its present. What they cannot know, between hurried round trip flights from New York or Los Angeles, is that WCCO Radio fits its listeners as snugly, as warmly, as a favorite stocking cap on a winter night. At its best, it is radio without pretense: communicating simply, informally, honestly. "Companion" comes from the Latin for "with bread." Good radio certainly is a companion that has earned its place in the kitchen, where bread is broken. WCCO Radio compels listeners to think, react, and certainly, to buy. Perhaps WCCO Radio veteran Gordon Mikkelson, man of a thousand ideas, put it

CBS President Thomas Wyman with former WCCO Radio Vice President and General Manager Phil Lewis: "People ask me what I miss most about Minnesota...and I say... I think it's the school closings. There is more wit and intellect on WCCO than any radio station in the country."

Thomas Wyman
President
CBS, Inc.

CBS News Correspondent Harry Reasoner and Howard Viken, 1982, recalling their early morning hours together in the early 1950's. Viken was a rookie announcer, Reasoner a newswriter told by WCCO management that he didn't have the voice to be a newscaster.

101

best years earlier, "We're great believers in building audiences by 'ones'...it means treating our listeners with consideration and respect."

There was, to be sure, more to WCCO Radio in the 1980's than character voices. It took important steps in news and public service. It became part, for the first time, of a fully equipped Weather Center, with some of the finest meteorologists in the area including Bill Endersen, Mike Lynch and Milt Lefebvre, staffing the center 24 hours a day, seven days a week. It has built the finest radio news bureau in the region, with veterans Rich Holter, Bruce Hagevik, Jan Falstad, Eric Eskola, Steve Murphy, Jan Jirak and Judy Hutterer. Murphy's 1983 series on a young woman who died waiting for a heart transplant captured the station's fifth Peabody award. In 1982, WCCO followed the melancholy journey of the replica of the Viking ship Hjemkomst from Duluth to Bergen, Norway, News Director Curt Beckmann

and reporter Eskola conveying vivid sound images of the ship's arrival in a Norwegian harbor. WCCO attracted nationwide attention when it hired as its traffic reporter, a young man named Dean Spratt, legally blind since birth, who surrounded himself with squawking dispatch radios, delivering rush hour traffic reports with accuracy and wit.

In 1983, WCCO Radio was a major sponsor with WCCO-TV for Metro Foodshare, an unprecedented campaign of public and private sector cooperation, to replenish emergency foodshelves in the greater Twin Cities area. Fueled by a matching challenge of 100,000 pounds from the Pillsbury Company, the campaign aimed for a goal in February, 1983 of 200,000 pounds of donated food from WCCO listeners. The final figure: 1,700,000 pounds for the hungry poor of the Twin Cities and the Iron Range, including more than a third of a million dollars in cash contributions. The following year, with the help of the Greater Minneapolis Council of Churches, the program went statewide as Minnesota Foodshare, aimed for 2,000,000, and went 700,000 pounds over its goal.

At almost the same time, WCCO Radio helped organize, promote and broadcast the first major marathon in the Twin Cities. For years, Saint Paul and Minneapolis had smaller races. Veteran

Boone and Erickson, music madmen, clowning for the St. Paul Chamber Orchestra.

WCCO Radio News Director Curt Beckmann, second left, Newsman Steve Murphy, center, and General Manager Clayt Kaufman, second right, accept WCCO Radio's fifth Peabody Award, 1984, New York City, for Murphy's series, "Debbie Peilow: Waiting for a Heart That Never Came."

"*Fitness does not add to life in the future,*" wrote George Sheehan, "*but adds to life today.*" In the 1980's, WCCO Radio led the fitness and running revolution in the region. Above, Alan Zachariason of Denmark wins the first Twin Cities Marathon, hitting the tape at the finish line in Saint Paul. Above, right, the start at the Pillsbury Center in downtown Minneapolis. And right, WCCO Radio fitness and running expert, Dick Beardsley, of Rush City, Minnesota, one of the world's top marathoners.

Brent: *I'm wearing number 13 and this is my 13th marathon!*

Erickson: *It's a lucky number for you. You were really lit up when you crossed that finish line. That must be a great feeling.*

Brent: *It is. It was a great feeling from 18 miles on.*

Boone: *How'd you feel when you passed most of the guys?*

Brent: *That's a pretty good feeling.*

Boone: *Did you wave at them as you passed by?*

Brent: *No! They don't like that!*

Sally Brent, Sioux City, Iowa,
winner of the 1982 Twin Cities Marathon
with Boone and Erickson on WCCO Radio
the finish line. October 3, 1982

marathoner Jack Moran, a University of Minnesota associate professor of aeronautical engineering, felt the time had come for the two cities to share a marathon course. WCCO Radio put its full promotional muscle behind the race. One morning in early 1982, Chief Executive Officer William Spoor of Pillsbury heard one of the promotional spots for the Twin Cities Marathon on WCCO Radio while driving to work. Within a week, Pillsbury committed $30,000 to help finance the marathon (after original seed money of $20,000 from Dain-Bosworth/IGF). Close to 4,000 runners took part in what Moran confidently called "the most beautiful urban marathon in the country." One published crowd estimate for that brilliant Sunday morning in early October: 100,000, which would make it the single largest spectator sports event in Minnesota history. In 1983, it became the seventh largest marathon in the United States, almost 8,000 registered runners; by 1984, offering $150,000 in prize money, the wealthiest marathon on the Association of Road Racing Athletes circuit. WCCO Radio offered exclusive, live, start-to-finish coverage for three hours, a first for a Twin Cities radio station. It was an eventful era for football

Boone and Erickson leading the world's largest marching band, Minneapolis, 1982.

"Now, these gags are not funny on paper. Nor are most of the one-, two-, or three-liners that will be told on the show today or any other day, often as the tellers themselves grimace in acknowledgement that the material is corny, predictable, even dated. A television comic would not last 15 minutes on this stuff. But it is funny, often very funny, on the radio....It is the old magic of radio..."

Ron Meador
on Boone and Erickson
The Minneapolis Tribune
March 8, 1981

Ruth Koscielak

and baseball too: the arrival of the evangelical Lou Holtz to revive a foundering Gopher football program, the demise of Met Stadium in Bloomington, the construction of the Metrodome, the $32,000,000 sale of Calvin and Thelma Griffith's controlling interest in the Minnesota Twins to Minneapolis banker Carl Pohlad.

NEW PERSONALITIES approached a WCCO Radio microphone for the first time, by chance, and design. By chance came the witty, unpredictable Saint Paul newspaperman, Bill Farmer, who burst on the scene one quiet September morning in 1981 as a guest host on the *Boone and Erickson Show* and quickly became a raucous fixture on the *Top of the Morning Show* from 6-7 a.m. By design, came two Saint Paul natives. Twenty-six-year-old Ruth Koscielak, won listeners with her open, accepting voice and stylish taste in music.

Friends of the WCCO Radio Family, 1984: top row left to right, Twin Cities internist, Dr. William A. O'Brien; Dave Mona, host of the Sunday morning Sports Huddle *with Sid Hartman; food and wine expert Jack Farrell; second row, Ginger Sisco, director of the Minnesota Tourism Department; Dr. Leon Snyder, professor emeritus, horticulture, University of Minnesota; real estate expert Dr. George Karvel of Saint Cloud State,* Sunday Punch; *third row: story teller-essayist Jergen Nash,* Sunday Punch; *Movie reviewer Jim Delmont,* Sunday Punch; *and WCCO Radio's consulting naturalist-phenologist, Jim Gilbert; bottom row: Deborah Brown, University of Minnesota lawn and garden expert; Paul Flatley, co-host of the Minnesota Vikings* Feedback Show; *Michael Fedo, fitness and running expert.*

Roger Erickson and Charles Osgood of CBS News, 1981.

The second: the reticent Tim Russell, impressionist (George Patton, John Wayne, George Burns, Jimmy Stewart, Howard Cosell, Ronald Reagan, Richard Nixon, et. al.) and commercial voice artist. Their 1-3 p.m. weekday show soon had listeners recalling the early days in the 1960's of Charlie Boone and Roger Erickson.

By Spring, 1984, Arbitron diary samples showed WCCO Radio the number one major market station in the nation, in share of metro audience, 20.9 percent. It could also claim expanded efforts to originate live broadcasts throughout its primary service area and beyond. In a year's time, it broadcast, for example, *The Boone and Erickson Show,* everywhere from Saint Cloud, Minnesota to London, England.

"Your listening audience is absolutely fantastic. I've had thousands of people say 'Hey, I've heard you on the radio' and WCCO is the only radio station I'm on. I don't know if you realize how powerful you are."

Lou Holtz
University of Minnesota head football coach
on WCCO Radio May 16, 1984

"Five seconds left. First down on the Cleveland 46. Three wide receivers. Kramer back to pass. He's going deep. Down the right side! And…it's fought for…and…touchdown! Touchdown! Rashad! Rashad! Touchdown! The ball batted in the air and Rashad caught it for a touchdown! I don't believe it! I don't believe it!"

Ray Scott, WCCO Radio
December 14, 1980
Minnesota Vikings 28
Cleveland Browns 23
Metropolitan Stadium, Bloomington

Former Minnesota Viking Head Coach Bud Grant, just fishin', on a WCCO Radio MTC bus board, 1984.

106

Behind all this remain justifiable doubts about the future of AM radio. Will generations which listen almost exclusively to FM radio make AM extinct? The answer seems to have *less* to do with the way a radio wave is modulated, and *more* to do with what those waves convey to a listener. Perhaps it is more appropriate to ask, is WCCO Radio something a listener can do without? The challenge the next 60 years will be a twist of the old adage, "know thyself;" namely, know thy listener. Among the thousands of letters to WCCO Radio in 1983 was one from a listener who identified himself as a "24-year-old, newly-married, newly-graduated and employed 'CCO fan." It said in part, "For me, 'CCO is breakfast at home, listening for school closing announcements, suppertime with my family, doing dishes with Cannon in the background. I'll bet if you asked, you'd find a lot of third and fourth generation 'CCO addicts…I know I'm one. Why give up something that makes you feel this good and is legal besides?" The movement of the clock's second hand seems to be repeating.

Only the human imagination can do justice to the Cannon family, but this portrait remains the most ambitious attempt to translate them to print. Left, Cannon's real life meteorologist friend, Mike Lynch, prepares for a live broadcast one winter afternoon just before lift off in a hot air balloon gondola in Saint Paul, 1983.

The Human Touch

Sixty Years Strong

Charlie Boone

There is a great need for the Charles Everett Boones of this world. If for no other reason than to make certain that the John Roger Ericksons do not take control of the insane asylum. Contrast, after all, is the essence of humor. Contrast made Laurel and Hardy, Abbott and Costello, Martin and Lewis, Hope and Crosby. Contrast helped make Boone and Erickson, after 25 years together on WCCO, one of the legends (in their own minds) of American radio.

It would be nice if WCCO Radio's enlightened management could claim credit for this ingenious, durable team. The embarrassing truth is it was an accident. Each man, to be sure, was carefully chosen for WCCO Radio, but they came together by chance around three o'clock on week-day afternoons in 1959 when their shows overlapped. Not until a major sponsor (Miracle White) expressed commercial interest in them did it become obvious that Boone and Erickson were a saleable commodity.

Charlie Boone is a native of New-foundland, the son of a diligent country pastor of less-than-modest means who traveled the rural church circuit in central Minnesota. Charlie

and his twin sister were part of a family of eight, living on the collection plate and farmers' donations of food and meat. He is today in many ways what his father was: histrionic, charming, a man who carries himself with a certain squirely dignity. He is a bibliophile who haunts used book-stores, sensitive to music and personal relationships. "I think probably the overriding influence on my life," he was quoted ten years ago, "...is either the desire to be loved, loving, to deal with that whole aspect of love. That sounds corny. But I really can't think of anything else."

Ten years later, that view of life remains, with new layers. His wife, Carol, a music Ph.D. and program annotator for the Saint Paul Chamber Orchestra, helped expand

his horizons. Her family and roots in rural Minnesota (Maynard, population 455) give him a new appreciation of the countryside and farm living. He shares her joy for classical music, she his sense of family. "I'm not as intolerant, withdrawn and hyper-sensitive as I used to be," Charlie Boone says now, "and for that Carol gets a lot of the credit. She's analytical, not prone to quick decisions and she's helped me be more compassionate."

The key to the success of the Boone and Erickson Show for 25 years? "Harry Belafonte put it best when he was on our show a while back. Unpredictability. As often as you can, give your listeners a surprise. Once they can predict what you're going to do, you've got problems."

108

Roger Erickson

Roger Erickson is a man for all stages. In the 17th century, he might have been Shakespeare's Sir Toby Belch in the "Twelfth Night." "Confine? I'll confine myself no finer than I am." In the 1920's he would have trod the boards as a Vaudevillian. "Did you hear they just crossed a dog with a waiter? What did they get? They got a dog that never came when you called."

Instead, in this time and place, his special stage has become the most imaginative of all media, radio, for he was raised listening to WCCO Radio during the Depression on a farm without electricity in the German-Scandinavian town of Winthrop in southern Minnesota. He did chores in the twilight era of the horse-drawn plow, clowned in school (sticking crayons in every hole in his head), studied drama and radio at the University of Minnesota. He worked briefly at a station in Stillwater, as Bozo the Clown on WCCO-TV, before finally arriving at the only station he'd ever really cared for.

After 25 years at the same broadcast address he has become the consummate radio personality: master storyteller and dialectician, the man who made school closings an art form, keeper of a semi-imaginary world centered on the Bernadotte International Airport, Air Lutefiska (advertising wider seats, unfortunately they're on the stewardesses), Charlie's Cafe Mediocre (Maitre d' Garson Larson) and a school closing summer camp for superintendents on scenic Lake Titlow near Gaylord.

After 25 years the zany magic is still there, the nervous energy, laughter as natural as breathing, the flawless sense of pacing on the air. No one can make an hour of radio move as smoothly, quickly and unpredictably as this man with the golden-gray hair, slightly stooped shoulders—too many hours over a beat-up manual typewriter—still as insecure as a weekend part-time announcer. Still desperately trying to prove himself every hour, every day. "Was it funny?," he'll say, after a skit. "Can we make it shorter? What about that line? Does that make sense?" Still up at 3:30 every weekday morning, still bouncing out of the elevator at 5:30 a.m., still hunched over the turntable in the record library, rehearsing a bit to the tune of some Broadway musical. Still darting up and down the corridors, bouncing an idea here and there, testing his latest story line on the nearest innocent bystander outside the studio. He hears an idea, a funny premise, and it's "let's go back to my office, gotta get this down on the typewriter."

* * *

The air inside the Redwood Falls, Minnesota armory is thick with the aroma of pancakes, sausage and brewing coffee. It is 7:45 on an April morning in 1984. A long line has formed already, testimony to a free meal courtesy of the local chamber, and the entertainment: a live Boone and Erickson broadcast. At 8:02 a.m. Roger Erickson can restrain himself no longer. He leaps down from the broadcast platform to warm up the crowd. 8:06 a.m. The high school band plays the Minnesota Rouser to start the show. Erickson runs up and down the aisles waving his live mike like a lasso. The applause and shouting and whistling is deafening. Radio the way 'CCO has done it for decades, the way no other station *bothers* to do it anymore, the way only Boone and Erickson can.

Steve Cannon

"I believe in the characters (Morgan, Ma and Backlash). After all these years, I don't have to think about the change in the voices at all. It just comes naturally. They're in the studio with me, and except when I'm broadcasting live in front of people, I never tape the characters. They're all done live."

Steve Cannon
Radio and Records, 1983

The story may well be apochryphal but it could have happened. It says as much about WCCO Radio as it does about Steve Cannon. A woman discovered that the man she'd been talking to knew *him*. "He's rotten, terrible, arrogant and an egomaniac," she said. "But what *really* infuriates me is that I've got to listen to him for three whole hours every day of the week." His show since has expanded to four, which must drive the poor woman mad. Listeners say they either love Cannon or hate him. Some confess to both. What most agree on is his virtuosity in front of a microphone. Few in American radio can match his tightly produced, intensely crafted style that emphasizes economy of thought and sharp wit. Make no mistake. He may call it *The Cannon Mess* but it is as deliberately constructed as an office building—each show carries his mental blueprint.

He was raised in Eveleth during the Depression on the Minnesota Iron Range, grandson of a coal truck driver, intensely competitive, sometimes contentious, the sort who'd never back away from a fight, who

110

would do things his way or not at all. Much like James Jones' Private Robert E. Lee Prewitt in *From Here to Eternity,* a novel he still reveres. That uncompromising view of life has drawn him a pinball path the last 30 years from coast to coast, station to station. He tried, failed (and survived) New York City; tried, failed (and survived) Hollywood. Then stations in Mason City, Stillwater, Bemidji, Duluth and Milwaukee. Leave-takings often painfully comic. At one station he yelled "I quit!" and the general manager bellowed at the same time "You're fired!" In the Twin Cities he bounced his acerbic way from WTCN-TV to WMIN to WLOL to KSTP Radio before finally landing, still the rugged individualist, at the Good Neighbor to the Northwest in 1971, where he seems, finally,

to have found a home.

The apparent arrogance, the insecurity, sometimes what some think rudeness, are still there, but so more often are the delicious moments of mellowness, forgiveness, honest sentiment, and self-deprecating humor (served up by Morgan, Ma and Backlash). Beneath the bombastic veneer is a man who places great value on candor, honesty, and the importance of roots and family. Someday, perhaps in the not too distant future, Steve Cannon may be ready for the crowning accomplishment of his checkered career: reading school closings some wicked winter afternoon as if he meant every word. Only then would he really be able to consider that final job at KBUM Radio in Baudette, Minnesota with true peace of mind.

Howard Viken

To hear Howard Viken tell it, just about everyone else at WCCO Radio over the years has been responsible for his success except him. The senior announcers, when he first started at 'CCO in 1950, were "like fathers to me." The management that was "never down on your neck, but kept encouraging me to be myself and have fun on the air." His colleagues today who "support one another, like any family we bicker once in awhile but when it really matters we come to each other's rescue."

This is all very fine and it *is* true but it reveals almost nothing about Howard Viken other than that he is a nice guy. Viken remains a somewhat private person, not stand-offish but in a polite, decorous, gentlemanly way. Almost unfailingly courteous and agreeable. He saves that private side of himself only for special occasions and special people, which is to say his listeners and his weekday show. On the air speaking to thousands and yet speaking only one to one, he can be the most intimate human being one could ever hope to hear. His style is almost unfailingly consistent: the disarming chuckle, the devilish tip-toe around a naughty joke, the very honorable sense of knowing exactly in any situation, spontaneous or otherwise, what is in good taste. Friendly, but not overdoing it. Pleasant but not *too* pleasant. Silly but in small doses. Informative but not pedantic. Fluffing a word here and there and knowing when to dwell on it and when not. Witty, but drawing attention to the subject, not himself. Viken's tool for this precise art is one of the best radio voices in America, deep, mellow, with a playful lyric pleasantness.

When he reads commercial copy, every word counts, especially end consonants which he carves with an artisan's care, chopping his straightened hand in the air in front of the mike as if he were dicing each syllable like a Japanese chef.

His success springs from his provincialism. He grew up in North Minneapolis during the Depression, living in four or five houses in about a dozen years, attending several elementary schools, learning how to adapt and make new friends. His parents endowed him with their sense of humor. He recalls with special fondness the night his mother took the stage at some local civic performance and revealed, to his surprise, her hidden ability as a comedienne. He spent three years in the Marines during World War II, in combat at age 19 on Guam and Iwo Jima. After two years in speech and journalism at the University of Minnesota, Dr. E.W. Ziebarth suggested he attend Brown Institute, a broadcasters' school which had just opened in Minneapolis. He spent two years with smaller stations in Iron Mountain, Michigan, Duluth and Minneapolis before joining WCCO Radio. What has served him well is his ability to sell, everything over the years from savings and loans to Swedish toothpaste to, one year, German cuckoo clocks, dozens of which turned out to be defective and piled up in the station's mail room. He has, for instance, been the radio voice of Lund's supermarkets since the late 1950's. "I still love the work," he says, and you believe him, "I still look forward to getting up every morning. Otherwise, heck, I'd have retired by now."

Ruth Koscielak
Tim Russell

"I think anyone in radio has to be a little crazy to do what we do. Just think about it—we just sit in a room and talk into a microphone."

Ruth Koscielak

She was raised in East Saint Paul, a block from Aldrich Arena where she'd often ice skate with her older brother John at six in the morning. She was the tallest girl in her class at Presentation Catholic Grade School, spent hours in her room talking into a Wollensak tape recorder, had a deeper voice than most boys. When she asked the operator for a phone number, the operator would reply, "Yes sir, just a minute." Fifteen years later that voice has taken on a rich, feminine lilt, one of the most recognizable women's voices in the region. The youngest of four children, Ruth Koscielak learned early that she had to use her voice to get what she wanted. She was graduated from the College of Saint Catherine in Saint Paul with a bachelor's degree in communications and wanted to write radio ad copy. She did that and sold air time at a station in Ripon, Wisconsin, and, almost as an afterthought, some part-time air work. After a format change, she departed for a station in Saint Cloud where she soon considered her parents' persistent advice: "You've got to get out of radio and start making a decent living." WCCO Radio, her career goal, seemed a distant signal, until Program Director By Napier discovered her. Three years out of

college she became WCCO Radio's first major female personality since Joyce Lamont. Her afternoon companion on weekdays, Tim Russell, is her opposite. She is extroverted, assertive, effervescent (her favorite saying one week on the air was "Hey, let's have a party!"), Russell is detached, reflective, piquant, the sort of boy growing up in the 1950's who might have spent hours alone in his room reading *Mad* magazine. As a teenager at Saint Thomas Academy in Saint Paul he admired the carefully scripted humor of James Francis Patrick O'Neill on KDWB, the subtle satire of Bob and Ray, and Henry Morgan. He never cared much for television. "Television and movies limit the imagination," he says,

"Radio takes that extra step to stretch it. That's why I consider WCCO Radio one of the last true bastions of free form radio in the United States." He says all of this in *sub rosa* tones, as if he's about to be shushed by the librarian. In front of a live microphone, though, the hidden lunatic emerges. The shame is that it took WCCO Radio almost 14 years to find him a niche on the air. After being graduated from Notre Dame and fizzling in law school, he got his first radio job in Dubuque, then spent ten years at the erstwhile WCCO-FM before making the jump. Some of his relatives, he says with a wan smile, didn't realize he was in radio until they heard him on WCCO Radio. In a way, they were right.

Ray Christensen

Enunciation. Clarity. Projection. Skills which many college speech majors struggle to, and sometimes never, develop. Ray Christensen, though he didn't know it at the time, learned them growing up in South Minneapolis in the 1930's. His Danish parents spoke their language at home, and he learned it and spoke it before English. When little Ray said "tree" for "three," his father, who spoke with a heavy Danish accent, would say, "No, it's 'three.' *I* can't say it very well, but *you* should." Thus, clarity, in a tacit way, became learned behavior. His mother was a gentle, shy woman, his father a horticulturist, a Minneapolis Park Board foreman at Lake Nokomis, who planted many of the now-doomed American elms that grace Victory Memorial Drive in North Minneapolis.

Christensen remembers with fondness growing up listening to Clellan Card on WCCO Radio, sometimes pretending to do play-by-play as a kid in the stands at Nicollet Park. He received a bachelor's degree in speech from the University of Minnesota, worked at KUOM while attending school, drove troop convoy trucks for the 90th Infantry Division of Patton's Third Army in France and Germany during World War II. It was during the war that he realized how much he missed radio. He became program, and later, sports director at WLOL, working there with, among others, Steve Cannon, and taught radio drama with Dr. E.W. Ziebarth in the University of Minnesota extension division.

In 1951 he began play-by-play broadcasts of University of Minnesota football for KUOM (the first year for free, the second year $25 a game), continued the games on WLOL and in 1963 at WCCO; all of which means that Ray Christensen has been doing Minnesota Gopher football play going on 34 years.

Today, after more than 35 years in broadcasting, he has cause for rejoicing and regret when he surveys American broadcasting. "I'm thankful for the greater emphasis on news and information," he says, "because we are an immediate medium and we still do it better, most of the time, than television. But I think too often today, we neglect the way radio can stimulate the imagination the way it used to. We should tantalize the listener, because radio, after all, is a *visual* medium."

Sid
Hartman

"Look, you don't have to kid me. I'm not a radio artist. I'm a reporter. And at the newspaper, I'm not a great writer either. I'm a reporter."

You can spot him on a downtown sidewalk, tape recorder, mike and notebook under his arm, darting around a corner, sport jacket flapping, fierce brown eyes set in some sort of private determination. He looks, except for the silver-gray hair, like some cub reporter chasing his first story. His figure still lean, gait still purposeful, pursuing stories like wild game animals. The veteran columnist for the *Minneapolis Tribune,* the late Dick Cullum, said it several years ago and it is still true: "Sid Hartman has the best legs of any reporter who ever lived." You can out-write him, but you will never, or almost never, beat him on a story. He will not let you because that is how he was raised.

He was the oldest of four children who lived in a house at 525 Humboldt Avenue in a lower middle class area of North Minneapolis in the Depression. His father, a European immigrant, had little formal education, made $12-15 a week driving a furniture delivery truck. He left the family, and Hartman's mother supported the children with a dress shop on Olson Highway. At age nine, he came under the care of *Tribune* circulation man Art Harlow, delivered papers on the pre-dawn run in North Minneapolis, acquired the nickname "Blackie" among the news vendors, toughs and gamblers of "newspaper alley," 4th Street between the *Journal* and *Tribune* buildings. He worked five years in circulation, was graduated from North High and Dick Cullum hired him on the *Times* sports staff, where he earned $23 every two weeks

as a sports copy editor. One day, when a snowstorm stopped Cullum from writing his column, Hartman was asked to do one himself. Later, Charlie Johnson hired him at the *Tribune.* "You had to really work for a by-line in those days," he says now, "you had to earn it. And you learned on the job. Today I'm probably the only writer at the paper or the only air person at this station who hasn't attended college or doesn't have a college degree."

In 1953, doing sports for WLOL at Gopher football games, he met WCCO Radio General Manager Larry Haeg, Sr., during a halftime at Memorial Stadium. It led to a broadcast career now in its 29th year with WCCO that has helped make him perhaps *the* sports figure in the Northwest. "I am a close personal friend of Sid Hartman" is emblazoned

on t-shirts, always worth a laugh at bars and ballgames, but his favorite line also has a kernel of truth: Hartman knows more people in amateur and professional sports in the United States than perhaps any other sportswriter. His creed is the relentless pursuit of information and the ability to make, keep and cultivate a trust. His longtime friendships with top sports figures irritate some of his younger competitors, who aren't accorded equal access, and who claim he is too cozy with his sources. But he seems to gain most of his information with sweat, not favors. The irony is that the man who for 20 years has been the host with predictable questions for "Today's Sports Hero" on WCCO Radio really doesn't have any sports heroes. He prefers to think of them as friends—close and personal.

Sid Hartman and Minnesota Vikings Head Coach Les Steckel.

Chuck Lilligren

He was only 14 years old at the time, but Chuck Lilligren remembers the moment clearly. The moment when he first became fascinated with radio. He watched Randy Merriman do an "overseas special" program on KSTP during World War II for American soldiers in the Pacific. Lilligren was born in Santa Monica, California, and grew up in the Loring Park area of Minneapolis, youngest of two sons. His father, a Swede bank accountant, his mother, more than half Chippewa Indian, who worked at Durkee-Atwood. They separated, but he prefers to remember their gifts to him: their sensitivity to the suffering of others, their wit and sense of humor, the way his father would sing him to sleep at night. After West High School and an experiment with pre-law at the University of Minnesota, he turned to radio, six years with a station in Marshfield, Wisconsin, two years in Worthington, Ohio, five at KDAL in Duluth.

For almost 30 years, he worked six and sometimes seven day weeks, raising, along with his wife Marge, a family of seven children, now ages 22 to 34. Along the way, on his uncle's farm in Mahnomen County, and during his Ohio days, he developed a love for horses, and today breeds Morgans on his hobby farm in Ham Lake north of the Twin Cities. His favorite is his first registered Morgan, a 16-year-old named "Farleigh."

His coverage of the Norman Mastrian murder trial as a stringer in Duluth, helped bring him full time to WCCO Radio in 1965, where listeners compared his voice at times to that of the late Cedric Adams. "I felt then, and still feel today that WCCO Radio is like 'playing the palace.'" he says. "If you don't care for the coasts or the networks, then there is no better place in the United States than right here."

115

Joyce
Lamont

"When I'm on the air I don't pretend to be anyone else. I'm myself and I talk to one person. What bothers me are those announcers, and they're not on this station thank goodness, who sound phony. I hate that more than anything else."

Joyce Lamont says she never wanted to be on the air and did her best to convince management at WCCO Radio that she didn't belong there. She would have gladly settled, she still says, for production and writing. But now, 36 years after coming to WCCO Radio fresh out of the University of Minnesota, she remains the most durable and dedicated member

of the station's air staff and shows every sign, thank you, of wanting to continue. "I thoroughly enjoy life," she says, "I almost never get sick. I love people. And I love my job. It's that simple."

She was one of three daughters of the director of the state tuberculosis sanitarium in San Haven, North Dakota, not far from Winnipeg, a sanitarium her father founded. She spent most of her childhood growing up on its grounds, a gentle girl, easily hurt, indulged by two loving parents.

Her early work at WCCO required hours of writing. In those days most programming was scripted. She came to the attention of General Manager Gene Wilkey after her first air work: a hurried eulogy of Dr. William O'Brien of the University of Minnesota, who, like his son after him, did features on the air on medical advice. Later came substitute work for Darragh Aldrich, and Paula Sechter, the Dayton's Musical Chimes

reporter. "In those days, Dayton's had absolute control of program content of that show," she said, "and it was tyranny. You'd have to audition *every* show the day before broadcast for their advertising executives."

Today, she commands more listener mail than anyone else at WCCO Radio, by some estimates 2,000 letters a week, requests for recipes, publicity or, often, fan mail. Her daily calendar of "Special Events," which some may think trivial, may well be, in an unpretentious way, some of the most valuable community service the station does. It is a soft signal to the station's millions of listeners that a community play in Hector, Minnesota is every bit as important as an opening at the Guthrie, that a book sale at your local library is the equal of the fanciest estate sale on Summit Avenue in Saint Paul. Day after day, week after week, it adds up. "I feel very strongly," she says in that voice of unmistakable delicate strength, "that it's very significant."

Dick Chapman

In the first place, Dick Chapman did not come from Missouri to Minnesota to work at WCCO Radio. He came to fish. As a kid in the Ozarks, he caught catfish and carp, came north for walleye and muskie and was hooked on Minnesota. Persistence made him a veteran trophy fisherman, persistence got him a job at WCCO Radio, after several letters and phone calls to News Director Jim Bormann in the late 1950's. He joined WCCO Radio in 1957, writing news for, among others, Cedric Adams. Then, one night, he was called upon to substitute for Halsey Hall on the 10:20 p.m. sports. His career as an air personality began. It was not long before he was doing newscasts during Randy Merriman's weekday after-noon show, which led to work with Merriman on the most delightful little experiment in evening radio in the station's history: *Honest to Goodness.* It began just after 9 p.m. weekday evenings: "Do you know the answer to *this* question? Who wrote these lines, "Candy is dandy, but liquor is quicker?" If you can, you can win $8.30 on 'Honest to Goodness!" There followed a quick segue to the show's corny theme and 50 minutes of phone calls to bewildered, amused or stumped listeners from Sioux Falls to Eau Claire. It was all punctuated by a mele of wild sound effects: breaking glass, clucking chickens, horns, whistles and character voices, orchestrated by an imaginary gremlin named "Abner" who night after night ably disrupted the show. It was an

early 1960's version of the 40's show *Quiz of the Twin Cities* but it worked, and even commanded, Chapman still claims, ratings to rival prime time local television. He was born in Kansas City in 1930, where his mother worked for the IRS, and his father spent 45 years with the Western Electric Company. A few weeks before high school graduation, he was the victim of a hit and run accident, lost his leg, his dream of playing football at Missouri and scrubbed plans for the Marine Corps too. He was graduated from the University of Missouri School of Journalism in 1952, and spent seven years in Missouri journalism before coming to WCCO Radio. In his 27 years with WCCO he has been a part of some of the area's most memorable news stories: the 1960 Democratic National Convention in Los Angeles (at which Minnesotans McCarthy, Freeman and Humphrey played major roles), the Fridley tornado of 1965, the Humphrey funeral of 1978.

Joe McFarlin

"I hear from listeners all the time who tell me, 'you don't seem to have anything against anybody.' I'm their only friend in the night."

All through the night, in that "real dark night of the soul," they listen to the friendly, chatty, mellowness of Joe McFarlin. A baseball umpire who used to live in Fridley, Minnesota, calls from southern Florida. He's listening to WCCO Radio and he's on his way to umpire winter league baseball in South America. Another listener calls at 3 a.m. to say he hears Joe "loud and clear" off the coast of Hawaii. All night long come the calls: Syracuse, Boston, Philadelphia, Atlanta, San Diego, Los Angeles, San Francisco—and Brookings, South Dakota, a farm house in Iowa, a cabin in northern Wisconsin, an apartment in South Minneapolis. Joe McFarlin is WCCO Radio's clear channel psychologist to the nation. It is more than good music and companionship. In his own quiet way, he is a life saver—it is very possible that he has talked more than one caller out of suicide—and who knows how many more lonely listeners coast to coast have been saved, literally, by his friendly voice in their sometimes desperate nights. F. Scott Fitzgerald spoke, perhaps, of McFarlin's listeners when he wrote, "in the real dark night of the soul it is always three o'clock in the morning."

Joe McFarlin was born and raised in Superior, Wisconsin, his father a railroad yard master, his mother a former teacher who directed the church choir. He played sandlot baseball with a contemporary from across town named Harry "Bud" Grant.

After three years with the Navy in the Pacific during World War II ("you've probably never heard the story—but I turned the tide of battle"), and speech and drama studies in college, he worked for KDAL Radio in Duluth. After five more years in Duluth as a children's show host on television ("Mr. Tolliver's Travels") he came to the Twin Cities for six years at KRSI, before joining WCCO Radio in 1967. He remains one of the few on-the-air curators of big band and swing music in major market radio in the United States. "There's a revival of that music today, and for good reason," he says, "it's better written, better structured music than a lot of today's rock music. Mick Jagger admits he can't handle 'Body and Soul.'" It's not unusual, he says to get a call in the middle of the night from a rock band member calling from a pay phone between gigs telling him how much the band enjoys listening to Bunny Berrigan or Bix Beiderbecke.

Bill
Diehl

per-sis-tence (pĕr·sĭs'tĕns), n. 1. the action or fact of persisting. to continue steadily or firmly in some state, purpose, course of action. 2. to last or endure. 3. see also: Diehl, Bill.

In June, 1941, a 16-year-old student from Saint Paul Central took over a delivery route of 84 homes for the *Pioneer Press and Dispatch* in his Highland Village neighborhood. He was not content with merely delivering papers and collecting accounts. He sold new subscriptions with

evangelism, often talking his way into the living rooms of bewildered homeowners, spreading the paper on the carpet, section by section, showing them exactly what they were missing every day. In two years, he had a route of 240 homes, attracting the attention of the paper's general manager, Hal Shugard, so astonished at the increase in circulation in that one neighborhood that he investigated personally. The numbers were accurate. Bill Diehl became a copy boy on the paper three months after his high school graduation. At 19, attending college, he became a copy editor, at 23 a Sunday movie columnist, at 27 the papers' movie editor, a job he's had 32 years.

He was born in Saint Paul and lived

until age 29 in a house at 1826 Hillcrest, where his mother still lives. His father, Frank W. Diehl, earned $50 a week during the Depression as a Ramsey County public defender. His son often watched him in the courtroom. Sometimes in the middle of the night, his father dreamed about his jury trials, waking at three o'clock in the morning and yelling, "I've got them! I've got them!", heading for a law book to check a legal reference that could save the case. He did private, sometimes risky, practice on the side, representing Chicago mobster Bugs Moran, and Frank LaPre, whose body was found with gunshot wounds near Lake Vadnais. Diehl's father sheltered LaPre's two young sons in his home.

Growing up on Hillcrest Avenue, he loved history, languages, newspapers and radio, with early memories of William L. Shirer's reports from France before World War II, and Cedric Adams on WCCO Radio. His radio career began in 1948, at WMIN in the Hamm Building in Saint Paul, then two years at KSTP-TV as a movie host, four more at WMIN, and ten percussive years as a screaming "top 40 rock jock" with WDGY. He made dozens of personal appearances throughout the region as an m.c. for rock concerts, with the Everly Brothers at the Kato Ballroom in Mankato, with Gene Vincent, Sonny James, and in 1964 for the Beatles only Minnesota concert, at Metropolitan Stadium in Bloomington. When rock began to grow sordid around the edges, Diehl sought respectability at WCCO Radio, where he began September 1, 1967 at the Minnesota State Fair broadcast center. He remains the master of groaning puns, Weekly Reader and knock-knock jokes, persistent pitchman for 15 years on Saturday mornings from Wally McCarthy's Lindahl Olds ("the popcorn's popping, the rolls are hot and there are bargains galore.") His personal library of some 75,000 albums attests to the range of entertainment knowledge. More astonishing is his endurance. He eats one meal a day, and has worked seven day weeks (except for occasional vacations) since 1950.

Bill Farmer

Fred and Mena Farmer's grocery store was at 14th and Main on the west end of Atchison, Kansas. On the proper side of the tracks but just barely. Son Bill not only worked there, he was practically raised there, in charge of the fireworks stand outside the building, and discovering at an early age that his father cared little for the state law prohibiting Sunday sale of 3.2 beer. Mostly he traded stories and jokes with the characters the grocery-deli attracted, such as R.C. Lassiter from Arkansas. As Bill recalls, his dad hired R.C. to stamp prices on cans of peas. "R.C.," someone asked, "how come you know what price to put on those cans?" "I just figure what I'd pay," he replied, "and add three or four cents."

Bill Farmer was graduated from the University of Kansas with a bachelor's degree in history, and came north to the Twin Cities ("motivated by hunger pangs mostly") looking for work in a larger city. Unaware of the city's ethnic heritage, he arrived in Saint Paul on March 17th, 1962, to apply at the *Pioneer Press and Dispatch,* delighted to find downtown streets filled with merry-makers in green hats blowing horns and drinking beer. "I decided this was the city for me," he likes to say, "It wasn't 'til later I discovered it happens only once a year." He toiled 18 years for the *Pioneer Press and Dispatch,* becoming, in the Saint Paul area at least, a widely read and recognized daily columnist. But that was it. On the other side of the river he was Mr. Nobody. That changed in September, 1981, when he appeared on the *Boone and Erickson Show* as a "guest host" (the ultimate redundancy) with Erickson. It wasn't long before he became a regular on Erickson's *Top of the Morning Show,* 6-7 a.m. weekdays, stopping the show with jokes and stories that delighted most listeners and enraged others enough to call or write to remonstrate

the Good Neighbor for hiring this snarling, sometimes offensive, curmudgeon. He learned to soften his approach and shorten his material. "Roger Erickson taught me three things," he says, "be quick, be funny, and if you can't be either, be quiet. I used to look at a *day* as a deadline in the newspaper business. He taught me how to look at each *second* as a deadline, like splitting the atom. Other lessons I learned by observing him, like disciplining yourself to keep your personal problems and mood swings off the air. And the listeners? They make the station. Television programmers often aim at the lowest common denominator. You'd better not do that at 'CCO Radio. It's not only a vast audience, they're intelligent and tasteful too. They call you on it, immediately, when they feel you've been offensive or violated good taste. They've given me quite an education." Farmer's now in demand as a banquet speaker throughout Minnesota and western Wisconsin. Not bad for a man who only a few years ago was terrified of public speaking and had hardly listened to radio at 6 a.m.

Herb Carneal

"You have to gain credibility with your audience, which comes through being accurate. Being enthusiastic at the right time, but not artificially so."

When Herb Carneal was growing up in Richmond, Virginia in the early 1940's he listened to Arch MacDonald do live re-creations of Washington Senators road games. Unlike other announcers, MacDonald didn't use sound effects to dress up his play-by-play, just a bell to indicate single, double, triple or homer. Carneal played sand lot and American Legion baseball but as a young man decided he wanted to be a broadcaster. What appealed to him about Arch MacDonald, except for the bells, was the honesty of MacDonald's approach, the way MacDonald preferred to rely on the listener's imagination, not contrived sound effects, to portray the action. It is a subtle point but it symbolizes Carneal's approach to his craft. When he had shed most of his Virginia drawl and got his first full-time play-by-play job (WSYR-FM, and the Triple-A Syracuse Chiefs) he did not use sound

Herb Carneal with the Elks Lodge Little League team, M.B. Hagen Field, Hopkins, Minnesota.

effects for road game re-creations, just the wire service ticker in the background.

After four years covering the Phillies and Athletics in Philadelphia, he did play-by-play for the Baltimore Orioles with the superb Ernie Harwell, who would become a member of Baseball's Hall of Fame. Chance brought him to WCCO Radio. He had done CBS-TV coverage of the Vikings inaugural year in 1961 and came to the attention of Len Johnson of Hamm's Beer, the Twins' rights holder at the time. He joined Ray Scott and Halsey Hall on WCCO Radio in 1962 for Twins coverage and has been with 'CCO ever since, missing only about a dozen games in those 22 years. He was in the broadcast booth the evening of Friday, June 22, 1984, when Twins owner Calvin Griffith and his sister Thelma Haynes signed over their majority interest in the team to Minneapolis banker Carl Pohlad before a Twins-White Sox game. It was the end of an era not only for the Griffiths, but for Carneal, who as a boy in Richmond adopted Clark Griffith's Senators as his team. "Calvin Griffith had a great

knack for evaluating baseball talent," he said shortly after, "perhaps better than just about anyone else in baseball. I enjoyed the Griffiths because they are baseball people, and there aren't many of those people left." The same might be said of Herbert Carneal.

Joe Angel

"I learned to follow instructions and admire greatness at an early age. I was quarterback at Galileo High School in San Francisco for a backfield that included O.J. Simpson."

Joe Angel moved so smoothly into the broadcast booth with veteran Herb Carneal this year it seemed he'd been there years. "He anticipates well," wrote one critic, a month after Angel arrived, "...when the game is on the line, or when the action is complicated and interesting, Angel excels at pulling apart the components and putting them back together in a way that gives the listener a clear idea of what happened."

He's a native of Bogota, Colombia, was a fan of Ernie Banks and Billy Williams with the Cubs when he lived in Chicago as a boy. He began his broadcast career in San Bernardino, California at age 21, spent four years at KCBS, San Francisco, became sports director at KSFO, and did Stanford play-by-play, Giants baseball with Lon Simmons and Al Michaels, and Oakland A's telecasts with former Minnesota Twin Harmon Killebrew.

Denny Long

He began collecting records when he was in the fourth or fifth grade, listened to the original Hank Williams offerings and bought one of the first Elvis 45 rpm's on the Sun label. He grew up in a house in Northeast Minneapolis, a block from Columbia Heights, across the street from Immaculate Conception Grade School. He would haul his little phonograph onto the front steps of the house and play records. "I must have been," he says now, "one of the pioneers in disco and ghetto blasting." It was a short step from that to collecting George Shearing and Ahmad Jamal albums, playing the ukelele around the house to his father's banjo, and loving just about any kind of music. He endured, even thrived at times, on the discipline and regimentation of the Christian Brothers at De La Salle High School on Nicollet Island, took a year of speech and theater at the University of Minnesota, attended Brown Institute, then returned for a Spanish major at Minnesota. After seven years at smaller stations from Webster City, Iowa and Owatonna to the Twin Cities, he made the jump to WCCO Radio in 1971 as music director for the new FM effort. When FM went its way, Denny Long stayed where his heart was, with WCCO Radio. His contemporary manner has become a fixture on the air and behind the scenes, as music director. He admits to a change in his view of life as recently as a year ago, a turn that probably took several years to shape. "I'm more relaxed and 'one to one' on the air than I used to be," he says, "perhaps because I've finally come to accept myself for what I am. Like Clint Eastwood says in those *Dirty Harry* movies, 'A man's got to know his limitations.'" His daughters, 15-year-old Tina and 13-year-old Angela are at the center of his life. "Some of our best times are simply eating out when we get a chance to talk. My goal is that they simply be able to do with their lives what they want to do. That they have dreams. All I can do is show them what is good in life, warn them about what I think is bad, and hope they make the right choices."

David Hop

David Hop remembers listening to WCCO Radio growing up on his parents' cattle farm near Baldwin in Western Wisconsin, on the transistor in the tractor, or a Twins game on the portable radio dangling from the ladder when he painted the barn. "WCCO Radio was the station I grew up with," he says now, "and there was no other station like it. I listened to Bob DeHaven, Cedric Adams and later Charlie Boone. I decided as a teenager that I wanted to get into radio and I can remember wanting to pattern myself after the sound of that one radio station because it was so different." Hop did the chores on the 180-acre farm, showed cattle with 4H at the Saint Croix County Fair, remembers big family reunions on the Fourth of July on the farm, hunting and fishing alone in the wilderness. After a year at Northwestern University of Iowa, and Brown Institute in Minneapolis, he spent 15 years at stations in Michigan and Wisconsin and Minnesota before replacing Franklin Hobbs on WCCO Radio weekday nights in 1981. His first show on the 50,000 watt, clear channel station, to a nationwide audience, was traumatic. His listeners made him feel at home. "I learned very quickly the staggering power of this radio station," he says. "It's one thing to be told that as a teenager, it's another thing to actually experience

the feedback there in the studio at night. I learned very soon, contrary to my seven years at a beautiful music station, that this is radio that people react to, get involved with. I try to suit that need by trying harder to share my home life, my personal life, with my listeners. If I can say some evening, "I was out mowing the lawn today and after all this rain it was like a jungle," then we'll get 20 calls from listeners about lawn-mowing stories."

There was a time when David Hop wanted out of farm life, but he is back full circle now, with the best of both worlds, living on a hobby farm near his childhood home with his wife Carol and their three children: Carrie, 13, Jodie, 11 and Steve 7.

Jim
Rogers

It was the sort of childhood, in the sort of neighborhood, that Grant Wood had portrayed so often in the cities and towns of Iowa in the 1930's. In fact, Wood was still teaching at the University of Iowa in Iowa City, when Jim Rogers was born in Cedar Rapids in 1940. Rogers was the oldest of four boys, his mother a school teacher, his father began as a messenger boy and over the years worked his way to vice president of Cedar Rapids' Guaranty Bank and Trust. The family couldn't afford a car until after the war. One of the rites of passage of childhood in the Rogers family was being able, at age six, to ride the city bus and deposit your own nickel in the fare box.

It took him ten years to get a college degree, not for lack of initiative, but because there seemed to be so many other things to do: touring Europe for six months in 1960, dabbling in radio at a 250 watt station, waiting for a military draft notice that never came (the draft board apparently lost his file). When he did get his degree, with a double major in history and philosophy, he became the fourth generation of the Rogers family to be graduated from Coe College. After four years with KCRG, he became adult education director for Kirkwood Community College in Cedar Rapids. Three and a half years convinced him he couldn't cope with the bureaucracy and politics of education, and he returned to broadcasting, spending 11 years at WMT Radio and TV.

To this day he's not sure why he was approached by the CBS Radio station in Philadelphia, WCAU, but suspects it might have been a seed planted by a Cedar Rapids competitor, Frank Magid (later of consultant notoriety) who may have sought to get him out of the market. He became part of the station's news-talk format, well suited for the faster pace of East Coast urban life, but lacking the warmth and human touch of the Midwest. He welcomed his homecoming of sorts in 1982 when he joined WCCO Radio. After a divorce ("it left deep and lasting scars") he's convinced now that only if he is happy with his work

can he be a good husband and father. "My number one priority is being able to do what I enjoy doing. I agree with those who say that real success is if you can get paid for doing something that you'd do for free anyway. Then, from that satisfaction I think flows the ability to build a successful marriage and be a good parent. You have to like yourself first and like what you do. And I like what I'm doing. In some ways I feel as if I've never left Cedar Rapids because the Twin Cities is just that—a big Cedar Rapids, progressive, wide streets, lively arts, hi-tech and healthy."

Curt
Lundgren

It's all there in boxes in his basement in his home in South Minneapolis, stacks of 45 rpm's and albums of British rock groups and the Motown sound of the 1960's, the music he grew up with. Some 5,000 records in all. "It was fresh and upbeat and new," says Curt Lundgren today, "and it was such a radical departure from all of the pop music of the 50's which came mostly from the same New York song writers. It really spoke to the people of my generation, the baby boomers, and it remains, for me at least, the most important music in my life."

Indeed, music is what attracted Lundgren to radio, watching one of his friends run a little five-watt pirate station out of his home. He attended Washburn High and Brown Institute, spent 17 years in radio before joining WCCO Radio in 1984. He shares his mellow voice with clear channel listeners Saturday and Sunday nights, does free lance commercial work, spends a good deal of his private time with his wife Debra and their two children, eight-year-old Jonathan and five-year-old Kara. "What really gets me excited about radio is when I know that I'm talking one to one with a listener in a relaxed and honest and natural way," he says, "When I'm totally myself on the air. And then knowing that out there are thousands of friends, at least I imagine they're my friends, who are reacting to what I'm saying and like the music I'm playing, and respond to it. That's what radio is supposed to be."

WCCO Radio News

Some television and radio stations are proud of reporters they send to the network. Such promotions surely lend prestige to a station. It can also be proven that it is just as valuable to *keep* good people as it is to send them off to New York or Los Angeles or London. WCCO Radio News is one of the few local news bureaus in the nation that has developed a reputation as a career goal for broadcast journalists, not merely a stepping stone for transient reporters who have their eye, or ear, on a network career.

"We hire the best broadcast news reporters we can find," says News Director Curt Beckmann, "then we do our best to keep them." It works. Beckmann, for example, is only the third news director in the bureau's 41 years, preceded by Sig Mickelson, who became president of CBS News, and Jim Bormann, who like Beckmann served a term as president of the national Radio and Television News Directors Association. Beckmann's current staff is a family within a family, perhaps the finest collection of broadcast journalists ever assembled at WCCO Radio. The proof is longevity. They have 113 years of combined experience in their craft. Senior Editor Rich Holter has been in the industry 25 years, former president of the Minnesota Press Club. Bruce Hagevik began his broadcast career in 1963 and has won numerous reporting awards. Morning News Editor Steve Murphy is a graduate of Rutgers University and won a Peabody Award for WCCO Radio in 1984. Reporter Eric Eskola brings a lively style and ear for detail and wit to his air work.

Government Correspondent Jan Falstad is a graduate of the University of Minnesota in journalism and political science, world traveler, already a respected member of the state capitol news corps.

Newcomers Jan Jirak, former news director at KFBK, Sacramento, and Judy Hutterer, a University of Minnesota graduate who covered the 1980 national political conventions for local stations in Minnesota, enhance the bureau's skill and depth. Its most distinctive contributor is traffic reporter Dean Spratt, the blind man who takes notes on a Braille writer and offers ten rush hour traffic reports daily from his special room equipped with programmable scanners, citizens band radio and three phones, in his South Minneapolis home. "Many people think because we can't see what we're doing, we're klutzes," he says, "I really believe that people unknowingly think if you're missing one of your senses, you're not all there." So much for handicaps.

There is more to WCCO Radio news than scripted five-minute newscasts on the hour. Those brief newscasts serve merely as a menu for any informed listener. As Eskola says, "We merely set the table, give our listeners an index of what we think is important. It's their job to seek more comprehensive reports." WCCO Radio programs at least four hours of scheduled newscasts daily, including offerings on the hour from CBS, the most respected broadcast news network in the United States, supplemented by daily offerings from AP Radio. Beyond that, something called "news flow" is woven into the station's sound, immediate updates outside of scheduled newscasts, casual summaries of the hour's important news, netalert bulletins from CBS, and "history as it happens," presidential news conferences, live reports on the significant breaking stories from anywhere in, or out, of the world.

Says News Director Beckmann, "Journalism is not perfect. It's the one profession which is subject to daily criticism. But it serves democracy well, when it is free, free to succeed and free to fail."

Seated, front row, left to right: Rich Holter, Jan Jirak, Judy Hutterer and Steve Murphy. Back row: Dean Spratt, Bruce Hagevik, Jan Falstad, Eric Eskola and News Director Curt Beckmann.

*Left to right: Milt Lefebvre,
Bill Endersen, Mike Lynch and
Shari Akemann.*

WCCO Radio Weather

The story is told with some nostalgia by quite a few people who have lived in 'CCO-Land for most of their lives. They will look off wistfully and say, "I miss the good old days, when Cedric or whoever used to say, 'Well, we've got a forecast here for North Dakota and it looks like we're going to get some rain tomorrow in the Twin Cities.'" No vortex. No upper level disturbance. No cumulo nimbus. No squall lines. Just a nice, educated guess by someone we trusted.

Despite all of the sophisticated gadgetry that has become the high fashion of broadcast meteorology in the 1980's, the razzle dazzle radar, satellite pictures, fancy weather maps and computers, it is still the human equation that counts. A broadcast meteorologist is still no better than his or her ability to communicate information simply and directly to a mass audience. Very quickly, the "weather junkies" of 'CCO-Land can smell a phony, someone trying to fool them with meteorological puffery instead of a forecast that makes sense. Make no mistake, the people

who live in Minnesota, Wisconsin, the Dakotas and Iowa know their weather. It permeates almost every conversation at seed dealerships, bus stops, coffee shops and drug stores. Not just because it's a harmless topic, but because the region's turbulent weather patterns affect almost everyone's plans and moods, even those who can only empathize with farmers who are continually at the mercy of the changing atmosphere.

WCCO Radio's Weather Center is staffed by some of the area's best broadcast meteorologists. Morning man Bill Endersen holds a B.A. and M.A. in atmospheric science from the State University of New York at Albany, and was raised in western New York State, fascinated at an early age by that region's heavy snowfalls.

Afternoon forecaster Mike Lynch, a native of the Twin Cities, holds a B.S. in meteorology from the University of Wisconsin, as does all-night staffer Shari Akemann. The dean of the bureau is Milt Lefebvre of Rice Lake, Wisconsin, who spent

almost 32 years with the National Weather Service before joining WCCO Radio when the Center became a reality in 1981. Lefebvre and his colleagues agree that radio still holds the edge over television in weather forecasting. It can update its forecasts and weather reports as conditions merit, up to the minute or hour if need be. Indeed, weather becomes a continuing, and endless, part of the WCCO Radio program day. "We have to do it not merely with accuracy, even though it's an inexact science, but with honesty and humor," says Lefebvre, "When we're wrong, we have to have the courage to admit it. Weather forecasting is a daily reminder of human fallibility."

Tim Moreland
Stu Voigt

Tim Moreland had spent some 15 years in sports broadcasting to achieve his dream: doing radio play-by-play of NFL football. His debut came not in Green Bay or Soldiers Field or the Humphrey Metrodome, but some 3,300 miles away, across the Atlantic Ocean, in a somewhat ramshackle press box overlooking the pitch at London's Wembley Stadium, where the Minnesota Vikings opened their 1983 exhibition season against the Saint Louis Cardinals. It turned out to be baptism by chaos. Moreland had no clear view of the stadium's small scoreboard, had precious little counter space for depth charts, and had to alternate play-by-play each quarter with KMOX's Bill Wilkerson, to accommodate a dual feed of the game to Saint Louis and the Twin Cities. An innocent listener wouldn't have known the difference. Moreland did a creditable job, and improved as the season progressed.

He was raised in Sioux City, Iowa, the son of a farm equipment salesman, a father who used to take him to see the Yankees play in Kansas City. Moreland had fairly conventional sports heroes as a boy: Muhammad Ali, Bart Starr and Mickey Mantle. He played semi-pro ball, received a B.S. degree in Business Administration from Benedictine College, Atchison, Kansas, and worked in radio in Wyoming and Iowa before putting in five years as the play-by-play voice of the national champion Nebraska Cornhuskers on KFOR Radio, Lincoln. He thinks NFL football today is as good, or better, as a spectator sport now than when he was a boy, with more graceful, specialized players, but he feels "the scheduling system rewards poor teams by giving them weaker opponents. Teams that should be eliminated mathematically remain in contention when they don't deserve to be."

Moreland's colleague, Stu Voigt, supplies analysis and color for WCCO Radio's Vikings broadcasts. He has been a part of the Vikings scene almost 15 years, drafted as a tight end out of the University of Wisconsin, and played on three Vikings Super Bowl teams in the 1970's.

Stu Voigt and Tim Moreland.

BACK ON THE FARM

Dear Dad,

I just wanted you to know how much Amy and I appreciated being with you and Mom over the Labor Day weekend. I think it's one of the best family reunions we've ever had. Mom works too hard, but what else is new? Litchfield hasn't changed much and that's good. The new coat of paint does wonders for the farmhouse, but I'm concerned about the furnace—it should be checked out before the winter. I think the most memorable thing of all was when you had a chance to sit with Amy on the porch Sunday night after everyone else had gone to bed and you told her about how sixty years ago this month Grandpa bought the first radio you ever had—the RCA Radiola…and how Grandpa let you be the first one in the family to listen on the earphones. Kids today think television's been around forever and they think radio is as old as the wheel. You've really started something with her. She wants to do a paper for her fifth grade science report on how voices travel through the air. Our drive back to the Twin Cities Monday night seemed long, we were both exhausted after all that volleyball, horseshoes and Mom's great cooking. Amy fell asleep in the front seat listening to the Twins game on WCCO. She doesn't like baseball that much but she said, "I want to listen to what Grandpa listens to." She was asleep when we got home.

Your loving daughter,

Emily

129

Allen, Frederick Lewis. (1931) *Only Yesterday*. Bantam Books, New York, 1959.

Allen, Frederick Lewis. (1939) *Since Yesterday*. Bantam Books, New York, 1961.

American Heritage, August, 1955. "Music in the Air...and Voices on The Crystal Set," Fifteen pioneers recall their adventures in the early days of American Radio. pp. 65-88.

Barnouw, Erik. *A Tower in Babel*. Oxford U. Press, New York, 1966.

Bergquist, J. Gordon. *Summer Boy Farm Life During the 1920's*.

Blum, John Morton. *V Was for Victory*. Harcourt Brace Jovanovich, New York, 1976.

Carroll, Peter N. *It Seemed Like Nothing Happened— The Tragedy and Promise of American in the 1970s*. New York, Holt, Rinehart and Winston, 1982.

Dunning, John. *Tune in Yesterday— The Ultimate Encyclopedia of Old-Time Radio, 1925-1976*. Prentice Hall, Inc., Englewood Cliffs, N.J., 1976.

Faulk, John Henry. *Fear on Trial*. Simon and Schuster, New York, 1964.

Gelfand, M. Howard. "Just Folks Radio," *The Wall Street Journal*, April 19, 1973, p.1.

Gould, Georgia. "Going Home with Steve Cannon and Friends," *Minneapolis*, September, 1975.

Green, Jeff. "Steve Cannon: A Man of Characters," *Radio and Records*, October 14, 1983.

Hallaren, W.O. "Radio is Worth Saving," *The Atlantic Monthly*, October, 1959, p. 69-72.

Hardman, Benedict E. *Everybody Called Him Cedric*. Twin City Federal Savings and Loan Association. Minneapolis, 1970.

Hoopes, Roy. *Americans Remember the Home Front*. New York, Hawthorne Books, Inc. 1973.

Jones, Will. "After Last Night: On Radio, It's Money, Money," *Minneapolis Tribune*, June 7, 1956. p. 36.

Ladies Home Journal. "How America Lives: Meet the Handevidts of Martin County, Minnesota." September, 1940. pp. 55-73.

LeSueur, Meridel. *Salute to Spring*. International Publishers, New York. 1940.

Lewis, Peter. *The Fifties*. J.B. Lippincott Company, New York, 1978.

Lewis, Sinclair. "The Long Arm of the Small Town," *The O-sa-ge*, 1:83, Sauk Centre, 1931.

McElvaine, Robert S. *Down and Out in the Great Depression*. University of North Carolina Press, Chapel Hill, 1983.

Mona, Dave. *The Hubert H. Humphrey Metrodome Souvenir Book*. MSP Publications, Minneapolis, 1982.

Perrett, Geoffrey. *A Dream of Greatness—The American People, 1945-1963*. Coward, McCann and Geoghegan, New York, 1979.

Perrett, Geoffrey. *American in the Twenties: A History*. Simon and Schuster, New York, 1982.

Perrett, Geoffrey, *Days of Sadness, Years of Triumph, The American People 1939-1945*. Coward, McCann and Geoghegan, Inc., New York, 1973.

Peterson, David. "Boone and Erickson." *Minneapolis*, June, 1974.

Putney, Michael. "Who Says Radio Expired with TV? Not Folks at WCCO, Minneapolis." *The National Observer*. June 21, 1971.

Saudek, Robert. "Program Coming in Fine, Please Play 'Japanese Sandman'," *American Heritage*, August, 1965.

Schaefer, Fr. Vernon J. *We Ate Gooseberries—Growing Up on a Minnesota Farm During the Depression*. Exposition Press, New York, 1974.

Sevareid, Eric. *Small Sounds in the Night*. Alfred A. Knopf, New York, 1956.

Shaw, Arnold. *The Rockin 50's*. Hawthorne Books, New York, 1974

Soucheray, Joe. *Once There Was a Ballpark*. Dorn Books, Edina, 1981.

Steinberg, Bruce. "The Mass Market is Splitting Apart," *Fortune*, November 28, 1983.

Time, "Robert Todd Storz: The King of Giveaway," June 4, 1956, p. 100-102.

Vaughn, Peter. "Going Home with WCCO Radio; Station Grows Bumper Corn Crop," *The Minneapolis Star*, p. 4C, March 30, 1976.

Wecster, Dixon. *The Age of the Great Depression, 1929-1941*. New Viewpoints, New York, 1975.

White, Paul W. *News on the Air*. Harcourt, Brace and Co., New York, 1947.

White, Theodore H. White. *The Making of the President 1964*. Atheneum Publishers, New York, 1965.

Wood, David "Alumni of Cedric's Troupe Hold Happy, Tearful Reunion," *Minneapolis Star and Tribune*, June 25, 1983.

Larry Haeg, Jr., 39, is the assistant program director at WCCO Radio. He joined the station in 1971 as a newswriter. He is a graduate of Saint John's University, Collegeville, Minnesota (B.A., English) and the University of Missouri School of Journalism (M.A.), where he wrote his master's thesis on CBS Radio's reporting of the murder of Sen. Robert F. Kennedy. During his eight years as a newswriter-reporter for WCCO Radio, he covered stories for the station around the region, as well as on assignment in Brazil, China, England, and the United Nations World Food Conference in Rome, 1974.

He is the author of *Heritage Northwest* (1976), a collection of portraits of historical figures of the region, and an unpublished biography of Saint Paul essayist Charles Macomb Flandrau.

He is the son of the late Larry Haeg, Sr., former general manager of WCCO Radio and former president of Midwest Radio-TV, Inc. He and his wife Mary live in Edina with their five children and 13 radios.

PHOTO CREDITS
(MHS—Minnesota Historical Society)
(MST—Minneapolis Star and Tribune)
Page 9 —MHS
    10—Engineer at master control, Mpls.
        Star Journal, MHS.
      —Oak Grove Hotel, MHS.
    11—Workers with equipment, MHS.
      —Dr. Paul Johnson, Mpls. Star
        Journal, MHS.
      —Mr. and Mrs. John Morton, Mpls.
        Journal, MHS.
    12—Studio interior, A.E. Kairies.
      —Mrs. Poehler, Mpls. Tribune.
    14—Donald D. Davis, General Mills.
      —Ground-breaking, Bureau of
        Engraving.
    15—Transmitter, Mpls. Journal, MHS.
      —Ground-breaking, Bureau of
        Engraving.
    16—Henry Bellows, MST
      —Studio broadcast, Mpls. Journal,
        MHS.
    17—Children/Studio, MHS.
    18—Studio interior, A.E. Kairies.
      —Memorial Stadium press box, MHS.
    19—Pianist, St. Paul Dispatch and
        Pioneer Press.
      —Harrington, Harris and Laws,
        St. Paul Dispatch and Pioneer Press.
      —State Fair Booth, Mpls. Journal,
        MHS.
    23—MHS.
    24—Tower construction, A.E. Kairies
    25—Towers, Bureau of Engraving.
    26—Paley, CBS.
      —Tower, MST.
    28—Toby Prin and Orchestra, George
        Miles Ryan.
    29—Studio audience line, MHS.
    30—Gilbert Orchestra, MHS.
      —Lamont Cranston, CBS.
    32—Bierman and Johnson, Mpls. Star
        Journal, MHS.
    37—MHS.
    38—MST.
    39—St. Paul Dispatch and Pioneer Press.

    43—MHS.
    44—Clellan Card, MHS.
    45—Hubert Humphrey, MHS.
    46—Youngdahl, George Miles Ryan.
    47—Haeg, South Saint Paul Livestock
        Market Institute.
    48—Union Stockyards, MHS.
    49—State Fair, Ahrend Bros., Mpls.
    53—MHS.
    55—Haeg, Kern and Dornsief, St. Paul
        Dispatch and Pioneer Press.
    69—MHS.
    72—Minnesota Twins.
    73—Minnesota Twins.
      —UPI.
    75—Minnesota Vikings.
    79—Freeman, Haeg and Johnson, UPI.
    80—Newhart album, Warner Bros.
    83—Erickson, St. Paul Dispatch and
        Pioneer Press.
      —Uncle Fogy, Camp Friendship.
    87—Shawn Weismantel.
    88—Guindon cartoon, MST.
    91—Viken, Theatre Graphics, John L.
        Anderson.
    94-95—Minnesota Vikings.
    99—Saint Paul Chamber Orchestra.
  100—MST, Kent Kobertsteen.
  103—Zachariason, Marathon start,
        Brent-Laurie Boutang.
  106—Vikings, Duane Braley, MST.

Susan Gilmore, 30, photographer of WCCO Radio's personalities, is a native of Omaha, Nebraska, a graduate of the University of Nebraska, Lincoln (B.A., sociology), and Brooks Institute of Photography, Santa Barbara, California (B.A., photography).She is a free lance photographer specializing in environmental portraits for business, annual reports and corporate brochures. She was the photographer for the 1984 children's book, *What Goes on at a Radio Station?* based on WCCO Radio. She is married and lives in Golden Valley.

Reed Merrill, 31, illustrator for *Sixty Years Strong,* was born in Minneapolis and raised in Saint Paul Park. He studied commercial art for two years at the Fargo, N.D. Area Vocational-Technical Institute, was a partner in an art studio in Fargo, and spent eight years with RKB Studios, Inc., Minneapolis before joining Dimension Creative Art Works in Minneapolis in 1982. He is married, the father of one child, and lives in Minneapolis.

Jon Quick, 30, director of marketing at WCCO Radio, coordinated production of *Sixty Years Strong.* He is a native of Eau Claire, Wisconsin and a graduate of the University of Wisconsin—Eau Claire. He joined WCCO Radio in 1977.

Design, layout and production by **Howard Burgdorf** and **Becky Lunde-Olson,** RKB Studios, Inc., Minneapolis.

A special thank you to WCCO Radio Business Manager **Bill Fuhrmann** for his thorough proofreading of the manuscript.

Sixty Years Strong is set in Times Roman typeface and is printed on 80 pound Vintage Velvet paper. It was printed by Viking Press, Minneapolis with the guidance of **Ken Sorenson.**